THE COMING REVIVAL

The Coming Revival

ANDREW MURRAY

Marshall Pickering

Pickering & Inglis Ltd
Marshall Pickering
34–42 Cleveland Street, London, W1P 5FB, U.K.

Copyright © 1989 Marshall Morgan & Scott Ltd
First published in book form in 1989
by Pickering & Inglis Ltd
Part of the Marshall Pickering Holdings Group

British Library CIP Data

Murray, Andrew, *1828–1917*
    The coming revival
    1. Christian life. Spiritual renewal
    I. Title   II. Series
    269

    ISBN 0–551–01865–8

Text set in 10/11pt Times Roman by Watermark, Hampermill
Cottage, Watford. Printed by Richard Clay Ltd, Bungay,
Suffolk.

CONTENTS

Chapter 1

The Conditions of Blessing

> '*Bring ye the whole tithe into the storehouse,
> that there may be meat in mine house, and
> prove me now herewith, saith the Lord of
> hosts, if I will not open you the windows of
> heaven, and pour you out a blessing, that
> there shall not be room enough to receive it.*'
> Malachi 3:10

The sense of a great need for revival is gaining ground in the church. Some are promising it most confidently. Others speak more carefully, and feel assured it will come, if God's people fulfil the conditions on which God has promised to bestow it. So we read in a letter of Mr Moody's, published not long before his death, 'If our ears are open to God's voice, and our hearts respond fully to his leadings, I believe we are on the eve of unusual revivals of religion, both in this country and in England.' If it is true that God's faithfulness in the fulfil-

ment of his promise waits on our faithfulness in the fulfilment of his conditions, it becomes us to ask most earnestly whether the attitude of the church and the ministry
is such as to give us confidence to expect the abundant
blessing we long for and speak of.

It is indeed a heart-searching truth that the union
between God and his people is so close, and that their
partnership in the work of saving the world is so real,
that the performance of their part is just as indispensable
as God's. Every one who prophesies revival would need
to be a man who has stood in God's counsel, has a divine
right to speak in God's name, and, in witnessing against
sin and interceding in faith, is fulfilling God's conditions.
Just think of a man like Elijah. God had given him the
promise, 'I will send rain upon the earth.' But how much
had to happen before it came. He had to show himself to
Ahab, to rebuild God's altar, to reform the apostate
people, to bring down fire from heaven, to destroy the
priests of Baal, before he could tell Ahab, 'Get thee up:
there is sound of abundance of rain.' And even then his
work was not done. He had to go up to the top of Car-
mel, and bow himself down upon the earth, and put his
face between his knees, and in spite of the word of his
servant, 'There is nothing!' wait seven times before even
the cloud like a man's hand could be seen. It is a solemn
thing to promise rain from heaven to a sinful people. It
needs a man who stands before God and gets his knowledge of what is coming from him, who stands boldly
before the people and pleads for a jealous God, and who
then in persevering prayer brings down the blessing.
Verily, it is not a light thing to prophesy revival, to give
assurance that God is going to do something new and
wonderful, to dare to say that he will in very deed 'open
the windows of heaven, and pour out blessing that there
shall not be room to receive it.'

The passage in Malachi from which these last words
are taken sets before us in a striking way what the conditions are on which revival may be expected, and what
man's part is in securing it. The prophet tells the people

that they have been withholding from God what he asks, and that he therefore withholds what they ask. God had his temple among them, as the symbol of his presence and favour, as the place of his service and worship. He asked that they should present their tithes there, both as an acknowledgement of their dependence on him and their gratitude, and also for the maintenance of his servants whom he had put in charge of his house. In that house God was to reveal and prove how he lived wholly to bless them. In that house his people were to show and prove how wholly they lived for him. God left it to them to show how much they would have of him. He would be to them what they were to him; he would give them in blessing just as much as they proved that he was worth to them. 'With what measure ye mete, it shall be measured to you again.' 'The Lord is with you, while (as far as) ye be with him.' And they had utterly failed. They had not brought their tithes or offerings as God had commanded. To show them the heinousness of their sin God charges them with having robbed him. 'Will a man rob God? Yet ye have robbed me. Ye are cursed with a curse, even this whole nation.' They had taken what belonged to God and kept it for themselves. They had withheld from his house what was his due; and God had withheld his blessing. 'Bring ye *the whole tithe* into the storehouse, that there may be meat in mine house.' The whole controversy with his people is about his house. If they will give him the whole tithe, all that he claims, he will give them all they can desire: 'He will open the windows of heaven, and pour out blessing, that there shall not be room to receive it.'

The jealousy of God for his house and service had been very strikingly enforced by Haggai a hundred years earlier. In the name of God he had reminded them of all God's visitations. 'Ye have sown much, and bring in little: ye eat, but have not enough. Ye looked for much, and it came to little; and when ye brought it home, I did blow upon it.' And then God asks them in one single word to consider what all this meant. 'Why? saith the

Lord of hosts. Because of mine house that is waste, and ye run every man unto his own house.' 'It is time for you to dwell in your ceiled houses, and this house to be waste?' And then when the people obeyed, the promise came at once: 'I am with you, saith the Lord. From the day that the foundation of the Lord's temple was laid, consider it – from this day will I bless you.' God's house on earth is the test of obedience of his people: in their devotion to it is the measure of their devotion to himself, and therefore the measure of the blessing they receive from him.

All of us who long for revival plead the promise in Malachi, and ask that God would open the windows of heaven, and pour out his abundance of blessing. Are we careful to ask, and then to say to God, whether we are ready to bring the whole tithe, all that he claims, into his house? Have we looked round to see if God's people, who pray for revival, are doing it? Are we giving our testimony to God, and pleading with his people around us for his house that is lying waste, while we live in our panelied houses? Are we sure that God will not say, is not even now saying, in answer to our prayer: 'Will a man rob God? Yet ye have robbed me. Even this whole people'?

'Consider.' What is, in this dispensation in which we live, the house of God? Christ spoke of it in the words of the prophet: My father's house shall be called a house of prayer for all nations. In the house to be built there must be room to fulfil the command: 'Go and teach all nations.' In the parable of the kingdom of heaven the king made a great supper and Christ uses the words 'Go out and compel them to come in, that my house may be filled.' This is the house of which God says: 'My house lieth waste: ye live in your ceiled houses.'

To the church of Christ has been given the unspeakable honour and privilege of building the house of God. Yes, believers are themselves that house, 'an habitation of God through the Spirit', in which the nations can be gathered in to worship him. The first work of Solomon's reign of peace was to build the temple. The first work Israel was brought out of exile to Jerusalem to do was to restore the house of God. The first object for which the church exists is to build the house of God throughout the world that 'every creature', these are Christ's words, may know the good tidings that God loves him. God has asked his people that they should see to it that there is meat in his house, that his servants may be supported and free to go and call all nations into his house. God has asked every believer, without one exception, with his whole heart and strength, out of love to God and his neighbour, to give himself to help in the building of the house.

And what do we find to be the case? After nearly nineteen centuries the larger part of the world has not even heard the tidings that there is a house of the Father open to them. After a century of missionary revival there are scarce 10,000 white missionaries in the field, as all that the church cares to give to meet the needs of a thousand million heathens and Muslims. Practically, throughout the heathen world, notwithstanding the attempts of the few to overtake the work, God's house lies waste. And all because Christians do not listen to Christ's command, and are not prepared to bring the whole tithe for what the house needs, to give themselves wholly to the work God has laid upon them. Missionary societies may plead for men, women and money; messages may come from converted heathens crying for more help; the Word of God may reiterate, command and promise; the great majority of Christians have not a thought of bringing the whole tithe into God's storehouse. Through vast regions his house lies waste; where it is building there is no meat in his house sufficient for the open mouths willing to receive the bread. And God's Word comes today to his people as solemnly and pointedly as to Israel of old: 'Will a man rob God? Yet ye have robbed me, even the whole nation.' Would God that Christians who pray for revival would consider the charge, even if they themselves are not guilty, and see how impossible it is for the blessing to come, until 'the whole tithe', all that is due to God, all that God claims, is brought into his house.

In Israel they had answered the prophet: 'Wherein have we robbed thee?' They denied the truth of the charge: they were sure it was not true. This word, 'wherein', is five times repeated in the book. Wherein have we despised thy name? Wherein have we polluted thee? Wherein have we wearied him? Wherein shall we return? Wherein have we robbed thee? The word reveals the utter absence of any sense of sin. They have no idea of God's claim, and how really he means it, when he asks the whole tithe. In self-complacent ignorance they boast of being God's people. Is the case so very different in our day? Is it understood among Christians what the whole tithe means, and that God does in very deed ask it? Is it preached and believed that with *the whole tithe* God means and asks the love of the whole heart, the devotion of the whole strength to himself and his service? Is it recognised that the claim of God is an absolute one, and that in withholding the men, women and money needed for building his house of prayer for all nations, he counts his church guilty of robbing him of that which he rightly claims, and greatly needs? God has a controversy with his church. Not so much with the lukewarm and self-contented who count it sufficient to be saved, and never think of the whole tithe. But specially with those who come as the representatives of his people and plead for revival. He asks them if they have brought the whole tithe and given themselves completely to his will and service. He asks those who by his grace have done so, if they have lifted up their voices and testified against this sin, if they feel its weight and burden, if they are prepared, before the blessing is poured out, to have the evil removed. God withholds his blessing, because we withhold his due. The very first thing needed before his hand can open the windows of heaven, is that 'the whole tithe', all he claims be given him. A great deal is often spoken about the lack of interest in missions that does not go to the root of the matter. Its terrible evil consists in this, that it is the proof that the heart is not devoted to God, that the spiritual life is diseased and feeble, and that religion is centred in self. Until the sin is known and mourned over, publicly confessed and condemned, and men are ready to be led by the Holy Spirit to a life entirely devoted to God and his service, prayer for revival will not avail.

What is needed is that those who see the evil should lift up their voice. Judging from what is spoken in many an assembly and meeting, council and congress, there is often a tone of mutual congratulation as to the state of the churches, which is so occupied with certain things that are good, that it utterly fails to recognise the tremendous hindrance that keeps the windows of heaven closed. It is only when bold testimony, and true confession, and deep humiliation prepare the way, that the blessing can come down.

How easy it would be, if God's Spirit, as the Spirit of consecration, were poured out, and Christians were quickened to give gladly and liberally, for every missionary society to double its income and its work, and make the three million of last year into six. A true revival in God's children would speedily work it. No one would feel the poorer for it; many all the richer. In seeking for the revival, we need to be made ready for this consecration, by confessing the terrible sins of the past, and pledging ourselves and our brethren to a new obedience. The Spirit of God can and will work it: we need to pray for the Spirit, with the desire and surrender to give ourselves to be wholly possessed by him, and led to all that God would have of us.

The prayer for revival is a most heart-searching thing. It brings with it tremendous responsibilities. It needs great divine grace. It asks if we are ready to take our hearts and lives from other interests and to bear the weight and sorrow of those in the city of God who sigh and cry because of the abominations that are done in the midst thereof. It asks if we so believe in prayer, in our right and power with God, as to undertake this great request, that God shall entirely change the life of some, of many, of his people from one of selfishness to one of entire self-sacrifice. It asks whether we will be the first to give the answer, to offer ourselves for the Holy Spirit to do his full work of convincing of sin and consuming what is of self. It asks if we will accept and carry the answer to our brethren and prove what God can do. Oh, this prayer for revival may mean much to us in more ways than one, but let us not fear. Let us unhesitatingly bring the whole tithe into his house; let us unhesitatingly expect to see the windows of heaven opened and floods of blessing poured out.

Chapter 2

A Revived Church – the Only Hope for a Dying World

> *'God be merciful unto us, and bless us, and cause his face to shine upon us; That thy way may be known upon earth, thy saving health among all nations ... God, even our own God, shall bless us. God shall bless us; and all the ends of the earth shall fear him.'*
> Psalm 67:1, 2, 6–7

In speaking of revival, and in praying for it, it is of importance that we understand what we really desire and ask for. To most Christians the word conveys the meaning of a large increase in the number of conversions. It is at once said: There has been quite a revival in that church or town.

The true meaning of the word is far deeper. The word means making alive again those who have been alive, and have fallen into what is called a cold or dead state. They are Christians, and have life, but need reviving to bring them back to their first love, and the healthy growth of the spiritual life to which that was meant to be the entrance. When the church as a whole, its ministers and members, is not living in full whole-hearted devotion to Christ and his service, is not walking in the joy of the lord and separation from the world, we need to pray, more than for the conversion of the unconverted, that God's people may be truly revived, and have the life of God in power restored to them.

It may be said: But is not the best way of having the church revived, to have new converts added? Does not that awaken interest, and gladness, and the Christians to new activity? This may be true, and yet does not meet the real need, for two reasons. Firstly, such a revival is generally very temporary, and very soon leaves the church settling down to its ordinary level. Secondly, these converts, when brought into a church which is not living in the warmth of the true spiritual life, in all holiness and fruitfulness, are not helped as they need, and do not rise above the lukewarmness around them.

What we need to pray and labour for, first of all, is that the church of true believers may be revived. What the world needs above everything is, not more men and women of the ordinary type of Christians, but better people, stronger in faith and holier in life, intensely devoted to Christ and his service, and ready to sacrifice all for the salvation of souls. When God's Spirit is poured out upon the church, and men and women, who are now struggling on in feebleness, are clothed with the garments of praise and the power of the Spirit, the world will soon share the blessing. They will be ready to give themselves to God's work at home or abroad; their word and witness will be in power. Nominal Christians will be judged by the power of their example, and will confess that God is with them. And the heathen world will, in the increased numbers, and the burning fervour of the messengers of a quickened church, share in the blessing. A revival among believers is the great need of our day. A revived church is the only hope of a dying world.

If our conviction of this truth is to be deep and influential, if by it our desire and faith in prayer for revival are really to be stirred and strengthened, we need the Holy Spirit of God to reveal the meaning of such words in the light of God's purpose. The spiritual character of the church, its great object as the instrument of God's almighty power in conquering the world, and the conditions under which that purpose can be accomplished, all these are thoughts of God – as high above our thoughts as the heavens are above the earth. It will need to be one of the very first things we pray for, that God himself shows what his church is meant to be, what he has promised to be to it, and how his plan with her is to be carried out. Let us try and think out some of the great thoughts of God as revealed in his Word.

The church has the charge of the world entrusted to it. When Christ had finished his work on earth, and went to heaven to carry it on there, he spoke of two powers to whom the continuation of the work on earth was to be committed. He spoke of the Holy Spirit, who, equally with God himself and the Father, should come in his name to convict the world of sin, and be a divine power in his disciples to reveal himself in them, and so make them witnesses for him to the ends of the earth. He spoke of his disciples as those whom he sent into the world, even as the Father had sent him. Just as entirely as he had lived to do the Father's will in saving men and women, was his Spirit to do that work too. And just as wholly as the Spirit was to be devoted to that work, was the body, the church, to be set apart for it too. The whole body of believers, and every individual believer, was to be like Christ, the light of the world, placed in the world with the one definite, exclusive object of enlightening its darkness, and bringing men and women out of darkness into light.

To do its work it has the promise of the power of the Holy Spirit of God. That Spirit is given to every believer to be within him the power of a divine and holy life. That Spirit is to be to him the seal of his worship and acceptance, the fountain of love and joy, the grace for conquering sin, and the world, the power to do all that God would have us do. That Spirit is to enlighten and guide and lead, to sanctify and fit for unbroken fellowship with a holy God, to reveal Christ the son of God the Father within the heart. He is to be a fountain springing up within, and flowing forth as streams of living water. In what he thus works in personal experience he equips the person to boldly testify about God's power, and to communicate to others what has happened to himself. Without the power of the Holy Spirit fully recognised and experienced the church cannot know or fulfil its calling. With him the life and the fruit God asks for are natural and sure.

When the Spirit does not work in power, it is proof that another spirit has been allowed to take its place. There are only two spirits in the spiritual world – the Spirit of God, and the spirit of the world. Between these there is an unceasing struggle going on. It is because Christians live so much for this present world, and under its power, that its spirit gets possession of them, and grieves and quenches the Spirit of God. They lose the power to conquer sin or live a holier life. They lose any intense desire to live for God and his kingdom. They lose the divine love that would enable them to live for or to have influence on their neighbours. Their religion becomes that of the mind and not of the heart. They are willing to listen to beautiful words on religion, and count the pleasing impressions these make as religious feeling. And all the while they are quenching the life in them into impotence and death. This is the state in which multitudes of Christians live, making themselves and their churches powerless for good or for blessing.

It is out of this state that a revival is needed to lift the church into its true life, according to the divine pattern.

A true revival means nothing less than a revolution, casting out the spirit of worldliness and selfishness, and making God and his love triumph in the heart and life. As every birth has its travails and its pangs, so this entrance of a new divine life in power into a church must be preceded and accompanied by the pains of conviction and confession, by the earnest searchings of heart in which sin is discovered, is held up to shame, and condemned. In such a work of grace many will learn how little truth or power there has been either in their conversion or their spiritual life. They will see things that they tolerated to be vile sin, that nothing but the blood of Christ can wash away, and the power of Christ can overcome. They will no longer wonder at some speaking of the need of a second conversion; the experience of many will teach them that the change is even greater. They will see that now, for the first time, they truly know what the power of grace is, what is the blessedness of God's love, and what the joy of a heart given to his service is. And work for Christ will be the spontaneous fruit of God's Spirit coming on them.

On those who believe that a revival is needed and is possible rests the solemn responsibility of preparing the way of the Lord in speaking to God and men and women about it. To God we speak about it in prayer. We ask him to open our own eyes and hearts, and those of our church, to what he thinks and says of the spiritul life he finds. We confess our own sin and the sin of our brethren. We give ourselves to stand in the gap, to take hold of his strength. We ask the Spirit to give us the consciousness of being intercessors, who in tender love, and yet in holy zeal and truth, speak to God about the state in which his church is. Not in the spirit of judgment, or self-exaltation, but in deep humility and the spirit of self-sacrifice, we ask God to show us if it is true what we think we see – that the spirit of self-will and the world is robbing the church of its power to continue and carry out the work Christ began. We ask God to reveal to us if and how deliverance can come.

And so we get prepared to lift up our testimony and speak to our brethren. It may be, not at once: the fire may burn long in our bones. It may be, not to large audiences, or with any marked result. But if our speaking to men be the fruit of much speaking to God, of real waiting on him for revival, it must tell. As one here and another there – this is usually God's way – begins to see what really is God's will concerning his church, and what the cause of her failure, and what the path of restoration, and what the certainty of the visitation of his grace, prayer will become more urgent and believing, and the blessing will come.

All this must lead to the assured faith that a revived church is a possibility, a promise, and a certainty. As in the individual and his needs, so with the church and the mighty change to be wrought in it: unbelief is the great hindrance. And faith can only triumph where it stands, not in the wisdom of men, and in the hope they have of revival from all the agencies that are at work, and all the progress they see, but in the power of God, and his direct intervention. It looks up to and worships the God of absolute omnipotence and infinite love. God can, God will, these are its stays on the right hand and on the left.

Yes, God is able! It needs but an act of his will; and his Holy Spirit, the mighty power of God working in his church, can give new life to all who long to receive him. He can work conviction in those who are resting content in external prosperity and human agencies. He can give the joy of the Holy Spirit, first in single churches, and then in larger bodies, and waken his people as out of sleep to see and consent and rejoice that they are indeed the hope of a dying world. And God is ready! As the sun pours its light and warmth on every tiny flower to give it growth and beauty, God's love is waiting and longing to pour itself into hearts that reach out after him. It may sometimes appear as if he waits long and delays his coming. Let us be sure, not one moment longer than is needful. We may depend upon it, with the utmost confidence, that if his children unite in praying for a revived church as the only hope of a dying world, he will hear the prayer.

Let us give ourselves to such prayer, intelligent, deliberate, intense prayer. I now venture to offer to God's children what I trust may be a help in this prayer for revival. I wish to begin with pointing out what is lacking in the life of the church, and what the causes are to which this is attributable. I then propose inviting my readers to take time and set their hearts on the pattern given in the Mount, according to which everything in the life of the believer and the church ought to be regulated. I shall ask them to pray very specially that God would give themselves and all his people such a vision of what he positively expects his church to be, of what he has promised that he is able to and actually can make it, that in its light the conviction may be deepened of how impossible it is for us to rest satisfied with what the church at present it. This will prepare us for realising the utter impotence of all human efforts, and the necessity for our looking up for a divine interposition. It will compel us to listen earnestly to God's Word concerning the almighty power in which he is ready to work, that in our personal experience we may prove, and may be able to testify confidently to others, that God does a new thing in the earth, that he does enable his children to live lives of holy and exact obedience, of joyous and complete consecration to his service. We shall then be ready to believe with a new intensity in the Holy Spirit, as he can fill the hearts of God's saints, and clothe them with the power which fits them for conquering the world.

It is hardly necessary to say how varied the elements of prayer suggested by such a study will be. It will begin with heart-searching, and confession, and humiliation. The Holy Spirit will show us what part we have had in the universal defection, even while we deplored it. He will judge in us things that have been tolerated. He will open our eyes to see what is wrong around us, and to come to God himself bearing the burden of the worldliness and self-contentment of God's children, who are one body with us. As we study and see what God has promised, and connect that with the individual churches or the larger bodies to which we belong, we shall feel what a solemn thing it is to offer ourselves as intercessors with God, and witnesses with men, in regard to the dishonour done to his name. The word revival will get a new meaning and fullness of thought; the prayer for it a new urgency; it will be a new demand for effectual prevailing prayer. As the solemn words, a revived church the only hope for a dying world, are borne in upon us and burnt into us, prayer and intercession will become a transaction with God, in which our utter helplessness will have to take hold of and cling to his almighty power, and our whole life become possessed by the thought that there is nothing worth living for but the will of God in the salvation of men.

Chapter 3

The Cause of Failure

> '*Christ sent me to preach the gospel, not in
> wisdom of words, lest the cross of Christ
> should be made void … I came not with
> excellency of speech or of wisdom,
> proclaiming to you the mystery of God … my
> speech and my preaching were not in
> persuasive words of wisdom, but in
> demonstration of the Spirit and of power:
> That your faith should not stand in the
> wisdom of men, but in the power of God.*'
> 1 Corinthians 1:17; 2:1–5

In our first chapter we spoke of the terrible sin of the
Jewish people in robbing God. They withheld from him
what he claimed; he withheld from them what they
asked. We saw how it is nothing but the same sin in the
Christian church that withholds the blessing of the
Spirit's working, and makes revival so needful. We

looked only at one single proof of disobedience to God's command, the neglect of the church to be what God wants it to be, a light to lighten the Gentiles; the refusal of Christians to live wholly and solely for the glory of God in the salvation of men.

We dare hardly say that this neglect, this refusal is wilful. Men do not know that they are called to such absolute devotion; that the perishing world is really their charge; that God refuses to bless them because they refuse to live only for him and their fellowmen. When we ask how it is that with Scripture so constantly read and preached, and with its commands and principles so plain, the truth is not apprehended, we are led to one of the deepest sources of all the evil and failure in the churches. The truth is held, is preached and received in man's wisdom, and not in the demonstration of the Spirit and of power. Listen to what our text teaches concerning this.

There is a twofold preaching of Christ and his cross. The one is what Christ forbade, and Paul therefore so emphatically rejected: the preaching in wisdom of words, in excellency of speech and wisdom, in persuasive words of wisdom. The other is in demonstration of the Spirit and of power; the proof of a direct supernatural divine working. Corresponding to these there is a twofold faith. The one stands in the wisdom of man, is feeble, and changeable, and ever dependent upon human support. The other stands in the power of God which has its root and its strength, on the part of the convert, in the personal communion with God and the experience of his almighty operation. When Scriptural truth is studied or heard, is received and held as true, and does not work in power, the chief reason is that it is held in man's wisdom, in the power of the mind, and not of the Spirit of God. There is nothing that so effectually makes void the cross of Christ and robs it of all its power as the wisdom of words and excellency of speech.

If we ask the question how it was that the Jews in the time of Malachi could be so ignorant of their sin, and so confidently ask 'Wherein have we wearied him?' 'Wherein have we robbed thee?' the only answer is: spiritual ignorance, blindness of heart. In the Scribes and Pharisees of our Lord's time, we see men making their boast of God's law, priding themselves on their attachment to Scripture, and yet rejecting him of whom alone it spake. Having eyes, they saw not. They had received the Word of God in their human wisdom, and remained entire strangers to its spiritual meaning, to its revelation of God's will, to its renewing and sanctifying power. If we ask how it comes that Christians now still can rob God, can refuse him that whole-hearted allegiance which he so clearly claims, and can live, not for the glorious work he has entrusted to every one of his people, making God known to their fellow-men, but for themselves and this world, the answer is the same: the spiritual ignorance of the meaning and power of all truth which has only been learned in human wisdom. And if we ask how it is that even the leaders and teachers of the church appear to have so little consciousness of the utter defectiveness of the Christian life of the great majority of Christians, and that even what is spoken concerning it has so little effect, the answer is still the same: the lack of a truly spiritual apprehension of God's claim to 'the whole tithe', the whole heart and all the strength in his service, of the terrible prevalency and extreme sinfulness of withholding this, and so robbing him of his due, is caused, above everything else, by confidence being placed in man's wisdom. Scripture is studied, its truth is admitted, is preached and listened to with conviction and pleasure in the power of the human mind, without the power of the Holy Spirit to make it effective.

If we study God's Word carefully we shall be surprised to find how many things there are which it contrasts with knowing, and what danger there is in knowing without its leading to that which it was meant to produce. Scripture contrasts knowing and believing. The mind can form a conception of the most spiritual truths, the love of God, the atonement of Christ, the power of the Spirit, can be be fully convinced of their truth and value, and so give them a perfect intellectual assent, while the heart does not believe them, does not open to yield itself to their all-controlling influence. Scripture contrasts knowing and doing. In the Sermon on the Mount our Lord warns against the danger of knowing and not doing. To his disciples he said: 'If ye know these things, happy are ye if ye do them.' James says: 'Be ye doers of the Word, and not hearers only, deluding your own selves ... But a doer that worketh, this man shall be blessed in his deed.' Knowing is contrasted with hearing. Just as there is a great pleasure in a beautiful picture of some interesting object, so the mind may delight in the contemplation of the divine realities of which the Bible tells, of the love of God, of the beauty of true humility or great devotion to God or man, while the heavenly grace itself is not possessed, and the possession is hardly desired. Knowing is contrasted with being. As the science of education is advancing, the teacher is ever more being reminded that his work is infinitely nobler than imparting a certain amount of knowledge, or even than developing the pupil's power of thought, so that we may be able to acquire knowledge for himself. The true teacher tries to instil into a pupil that character is everything – it is not what a man knows, but what he is, that is the real standard. This is infinitely more true in the God's school in which God his children are being trained. What we actually are, as humble, holy, believing, devoted children of God, is the only proof that God's Word has in truth entered into us and done its work. And knowing is contrasted with living. In each child of God, there is working the power of an endless life. God's own life is secretly striving within him. As the great work of education is to waken a child to the consciousness of its power as a living being, all this success of the Christian life depends upon the clear and abiding consciousness of a life from God growing within us as surely as the lily is clothed with its beauty by a power from him. The knowledge that occupies and pleases and at length satisfies the mind, without day by day leading to the faith, and the actions, and the character, and the true inner life for which God meant it, is the most dangerous of all enemies.

It may well be asked how it is possible that men should delight in knowing about what they do not with their heart believe, or do, or possess, and about what they neither are nor live out. There is a double answer. The one points to the expression so often used – the pleasure of the pursuit of knowledge, one of the most wonderful powers with which God has endowed man is the mind, with its power of observing and comparing facts, of discovering and understanding laws, and causes and effects. The exercise of every function has been made by the Creator to be a pleasure. One of the highest pleasures that man is capable of is when all the wonders of nature disclose themselves at the bidding of reason. While some men study science for the practical use they mean to make it, there are multitudes who do so simply for the pleasure it gives, and its elevating and refining influence. There are spheres of knowledge in which this does no harm. But in the region of morals, where knowledge reveals duty, the result is most disastrous. In knowing what they ought to do, in delighting to have that knowledge put before them, while they do not obey and perform, the effect is the blinding of the conscience, and the growth of that terrible folly of self-deception by which a man is satisfied, is happy in the knowledge of that which condemns him. It is for this reason that the true educationalist is so careful to distinguish between teaching and training. He is not content to tell the child continually what he is to do or be; he watches over him until he has helped him to do and to be it.

In the spiritual realm this pleasure in the power of knowledge is still more dangerous. This brings us to the second answer to the question we asked, how it is that men can delight in knowing about what they neither believe nor do; about a character and a life they do not possess. When a teacher seeks to train his pupils to obedience, diligence, truthfulness, he is dealing with a life that is capable of these virtues, and has their seeds sown in conscience. But God's Word and the church have to deal with supernatural realities of a heavenly life, to apprehend which nature of itself is incapable. It is because this is not believed or remembered, that all our Bible teaching has no larger results in training humble, holy believers wholly living for God, for the supreme and most blessed work of making God known to fallen men. In 1 Corinthians, chapter one, Paul speaks about Christ who was made unto us of God's wisdom, righteousness and sanctification. In regard to the latter all evangelical Christians believe that we have neither righteousness nor holiness of our own, and that we must find them in Christ, the righteousness through his death, the holiness through his Spirit. But they do not believe that, just as little as we have a righteousness for merit, or a strength for holiness of our own, as little have we any wisdom of our own, nor is our human wisdom capable of apprehending divine things. They do not believe that just as much as our heart has been depraved and our will perverted, so our mind has been deceived and darkened by sin as to spiritual things. They have the impression that if God's Word is heard and read with interest and intelligence, it will work out its own blessing. No mistake can be more fatal. God has said: As the heavens are higher than the earth, so my thoughts are higher than your thoughts. As little therefore as I with my arm can reach to the stars, can I with my human reason reach to the spiritual truth and power of God's thoughts. I can form conceptions, pictures, shadows of what he thinks, and so apprehend them with the mind. But to apprehend the spiritual and substantial reality, this I cannot, but as God is pleased by his Holy Spirit to reveal and give it into the heart and life.

We all know how little, while the Lord Jesus was on earth with his disciples, his instructions really profited them. What he taught about his death and resurrection, about humility and love, they could not understand. They knew what he said; but it did not enter their hearts;

they could not really apprehend it. When he promised the Holy Spirit as the Spirit of truth, to guide into all truth, it was that they might have a divine teacher who would, dwelling within them as their life, give them the actual possession and enjoyment of what the words contained. And it is only as the church of Christ, and the daily life of believers, the Holy Spirit dwelling in the heart, is honoured as the only, the absolutely indispensable, the sufficient teacher of God's Word, that the commands of God will be truly understood, and come with the power that ensures their obedience. Ordinarily when a teacher or reader of the Bible truth that has been accepted, wants to enforce it, he seeks by argument to deepen the impression that has been made. That impresion may be a very pleasing one, and apparently deep; it will not be lasting, unless the work of the Holy Spirit is acknowledged and waited on as the one thing needful. It is only and always as the Gospel comes to men 'in the Holy Ghost and in power and much assurance', that it will be received, not as the word of man, but as the Word of God, which worketh effectually in them that believe.

Let us now return to the question: Why is it that Christians have so little sense of their calling to live wholly for God and his work? Why is it that so many a touching appeal from the missionary platform, so many a solemn consecration address does not bear more fruit? Have we not here a sufficient explanation? There is so much speaking, and so much hearing, in which either on the one side or the other, or on both, the Holy Spirit is not honoured as alone able in power to make the truth and living in the hearts of God's children. Plead with men as you will, but by all that is awful in the fate of the perishing millions, by all that is sacred in the honour of God, in the blood and the love and the command of Christ, in the power of the Spirit waiting to work in them; the truths you deal with are so divine, so supernatural, so beyond our mind, that without the definite work of the almighty Spirit, little permanent effect is produced. Of all preaching of the cross, of missions, of the entire consecration to

God and his work that is in the power of the Holy Spirit, Christ has said: made void by man's wisdom. The faith which comes by such speaking stands with wisdom of men, and not in the power of God. And the fruit is according to the root.

What a work opens up before us as we speak of prayer for revival. God asks those who intercede to take knowledge of what the real state of his church is. If they are to feel the burden, to confess the sin, to point out the evil to others, to prepare the way of the Lord in doing their part to show God's people what they must ask God's Spirit to do, what they must be ready to part with and put away before he comes, they need a deep clear conviction that here indeed is one of the great hindrances of blessing. Because the Holy Spirit is not honoured in his teaching, the clearest commands of God's Word fall powerless, and God is robbed of his due. Let our prayer for a revival, for the outpouring of the Holy Spirit, begin by our yielding ourselves to him to open our eyes to see things in the light of God, to open our hearts to regard them in the faith of Christ's love and his mighty power to change all. Let us open our mouths wide in persevering, supplication to God, and in faithful testimony to our brethren to encourage in them the assured hope that deliverance draws nigh.

Chapter 4

A Worldly Spirit, the Worst Heresy

'Because ye are not of the world, but I have chosen you out of the world, therefore the world hateth you ... the world hath hated them, because they are not of the world, even as I am not of the world ... I pray ... that thou shouldest keep them from the evil. They are not of the world, even as I am not of the world.' John 15: 19; 17:14–16

'We have received, not the spirit of the world, but the spirit which is of God.'
1 Corinthians 2:12

In this world there are two kingdoms, contending for the mastery. Each kingdom has its animating spirit, in which its strength lies, by which all it does is guided, and

through which it holds rule among men. Everything we
are or do derives its character and its worth in the sight
of God from the spirit in which it is done. This spirit is in
each kingdom, not a blind force or an unconscious ten-
dency, but an intelligent power working towards a definite goal. The spirit of the world and the god of this
world hold rule over every child of Adam. The spirit
which is of God is the power of the living God, working
as a divine life in the hearts of those who have received
him.

The terrible sin of the fall consisted in this: that man
chose the visible, that which this world offered of
beauty, and enjoyment, and wisdom, in preference to
the unseen, spiritual good of God's will and favour. And
the ruin and punishment of the fall is that man became
subject to the power of the seen and temporal, that
worldliness became a second nature to him, so that this
world was nearer, and clearer to him, and affected him
far more than the God of all glory and blessedness, who
had created him. However little it may be thought or
taught, the greatest danger to a child of God is from the
spirit of this world secretly and unconsciously influencing his judgment and conduct. And one of his greatest
needs is to have his eyes opened to see what the world
and its spirit is, and how nothing can free him from it but
being entirely possessed by the Spirit of God.

The great power of the world lies in the very fact of its
having and working in us by a spirit. The things of this
world, whether we use the expression of what is God's
immediate creation in nature, or of all that complex duty
and power, of possession and pleasure which, under the
rule of God's providence, make up life, have their origin
from God, and their legitimate claim upon us. They are
not in themselves sin. But with the fall we and they alike
came under the power of the god of this world, and are
made into the kingdom of this world, with its all-pervad-
ing spirit breathing in us, and leading us, all unconsciously, to act in accordance with its principles. Under
the influence of this spirit we are born and bred. Our

whole human nature is under its subtle dominion. The whole of society around us, as far as it is not very definitely ruled by the Spirit of God, constitutes an environment, an atmosphere from which, at every pore, we breathe in the infection of a life that is estranged from God. And yet, because it is a secret, hidden spirit; because it has accommodated itself to the teaching and the worship of Christ, we may be utterly unconscious of the evil that is hindering and weakening our spiritual life.

It is to conquer and cast out and entirely dispossess the spirit of this world that the Spirit of God is sent into the hearts of God's children. With Pentecost the kingdom of God came in power, the kingdom of heaven was begun on earth. Men and women were to live an unworldly, an other-worldly, a heavenly life, superior to all the good the world can offer, and to all the evil it can threaten, free from all its modes of thought and motives of action. The altogether, even externally, unworldly life of Christ was to perpetuate itself in the inner circle of his chosen disciples and friends. They were to be so wholly given up to fellowship with the heavenly world, to wait and labour so patiently and perseveringly to receive the light and leading, the joy and strength their Lord could give, that they might be able to communicate to their brethren about that heavenly life and power which would enable them in their earthly calling to live the unworldly life.

Some of my readers have already been saying, But how can we influence our fellow-men if we withdraw ourselves from them, if we are to live such an unworldly life? Let us remember, the power of this world lies in its deceit. It is a kingdom of darkness. 'The god of this world blinds the eyes, lest the light should shine into the heart.' Satan comes as an angel of light; he can hide the spirit of the world under the garb of scriptural truth or Christian duty. It is owing to this terrible blinding influence of the world even in believers that they cannot see what God's Word teaches so clearly, that it is just they who separate themselves most entirely in spirit from the world, who will be able to influence it the most. As long as the separation ends in the desire for our own safety, it cannot attain the object for which God calls us. But when we yield to the Spirit of God to cast out the spirit of the world, we shall understand that the deliverance from its self-pleasing and self-seeking which entire devotion to Christ and the heavenly life give, is the very power that will fit us for sacrificing ourselves to others, and gaining power over them.

I have spoken to believers. The most advanced believer will be the first to admit how subtle, how deep, the spirit of the world is, and how utterly beyond our own powers of watchfulness or victory. It is only a heart fully possessed by the Spirit of God that can know its subtlety or escape its power. If it be true that it is difficult to bring home this conviction to individual believers, how much more so is it when we speak about the church as a whole. And yet, I am very deeply persuaded that as it is the spirit of the world in the church that alone hinders the Spirit of God, and makes a revival so absolutely necessary, and so wholly impossible too until the worldly spirit be cast out, so it will alone be by a deep work of the Spirit, convicting the world in the church, that a true revival can come and the church be fitted for doing God's work in and for the world.

And wherein now does this spirit of the world show itself, and wherein does its sinfulness consist? 'If any man love the world the love of the Father is not in him.' As the great and first commandment is, 'Love the lord thy God with all thy heart,' so the great and first sin is the love of the world which makes the love of God impossible. It was so with the sin of our first parents. And when John defines what the things of the world are, and what the love of them, we are at once led to think of that first sin. He speaks of the lust of the flesh, the lust of the eyes, and the pride of life. Man has body, soul and spirit. Eve saw 'that the tree was good for food': this was the seed of all lust of the flesh, the desire for the gratification of the body with its appetites. 'And that it was pleasant to the eyes': this was the beginning of all that delight the visible world, its God-created beauty and treasures, in which the powers of the soul and mind are occupied and drawn off from God as effectually as by more sensual pleasures. 'And to be desired to make one wise.' Man has a spirit capable of knowing and enjoying God. That spiritual nature was turned to the world to seek in it and its wisdom the knowledge of good and evil. And so the wisdom of this world, with its boasted reasoning about God and good, has become the great enemy of the love of God, and the chief source of that pride of life in which men content themselves without God.

In our Lord's temptations we have exactly the same three tendencies illustrated. First came the satisfying of the bodily hunger by his own power without waiting for God's will. Then there was the lust-of-the eyes temptation in the kingdoms of the world shown to him. And then the appeal to the pride of life in the call to prove himself the son of God.

And how is it now that these three great manifestations of the spirit of the world are in the church? I do not even speak of the power of the flesh as seen in the terrible reign of drink and lust in the midst of our modern Christian civilisation. But I do speak of the selfish desire for rich and abundant living, for comfort and luxury, that marks our Christian society as a whole, and the great majority of our professing Christians. How it keeps from all true self-denial and spirituality. How it hinders everything like true self-sacrifice for our fellow-creatures around us, or God's kingdom in the world. I do not speak of the lust of the eyes, as it is seen in the greed for money that treads down the poor, or in the materialism that measures happiness by riches, or progress only by that which is seen or temporal. But I speak about that subjection to the spirit of the world around them which makes Christians just as keen in the pursuit of the possessions and enjoyment of this world as others are, and makes a life of self-renunciation or heavenly-mindedness to be regarded as equally impossible and unnecessary. I speak of the wisdom ever sought in this world and in herself, and I ask whether the church of Christ does not give abundant proof that the wisdom of words and excellency of speech has very largely usurped the place, and received the honour and glory, which belongs only to the wisdom that cometh from above, the wisdom which God reveals by his Spirit to men who are not worldly-minded but heavenly-minded? Self-pleasing, whether in its more obvious or more refined forms, whether in those who are wholly given to it or only give it a partial submission, leads inevitably to that, often unconscious, pride of life, which makes the love of God with all the heart impracticable. 'If any man love the world the love of the Father is not in him.'

Our Lord Jesus was not of the world. He knew it and acted under the consciousness of it. He spoke about it to the disciples and the Jews; if they were to know him aright they must know this as one of the secrets of his inner life. He said to the disciples that they were as little of the world as he was. He wanted them to know it: without this knowledge their life could not possibly be what he meant it to be. Without their readiness they could not be prepared for the great revival that came with Pentecost. Unless in our prayer for revival we are ready to test the church, and to test ourselves, by this touchstone, our prayer will be in vain. With Christ his not being of the world meant everything. He proved it by separating himself from its sin, by exposing and reproving it, by accepting the cross it prepared for him as the proof of the distance between it and him. The cross revealed the spirit of the world, its irreconcilable enmity to him. It revealed the Spirit of Christ – his refusal of its friendship, his endurance of its hate and rejection. The cross is the everlasting symbol of the relation between Christ and the unregenerate world. What is called folly, he counted wisdom. What it called weakness, he proved to be strength. What it despised, he gloried in.

What is law for the head, is law for the members; the disciple must be as his master. So Paul understood it when he cried: 'God forbid that I should glory save in the cross of our lord Jesus Christ by which I am crucified unto the world, and the world to me.' There we have for all time the response of the true disciple to the Master's call not to be of the world. The cross proves how the world cannot understand the disciple, how the disciple dare not blot out the difference between the spirit of the master and the spirit of the world; dare not please the world or seek to be reconciled to it; dare not look upon the world, and its spirit, in any other light than this: 'I am crucified to the world, and the world to me.' As it was the separation of Christ from the world by the cross that gave him the power over the world, and gave Paul his, it is this alone that will give the church of our days its power. Just as far as we enter into the world, and please it, we lose our power. 'Not of the world even as Christ was not of the world,' we shall be able to bless it.

If it is true that the prince of darkness came as an angel of light, deceiving the very elect, that the god of this world blinds the eyes, how we need in the enquiry as to the state of the church and our own state to set aside all self-confidence, and to place ourelves very honestly and persistently in the very light of God, to have the Holy Spirit show us what the divine meaning is of Christ's 'ye are not of the world', and what of the spirit of the world, there may be still in us. The world seeks the gratification of self, and seeks that in the things of the world, and seeks it according to methods and principles which the wisdom of this world inspires and approves. In any of these three respects our religion or our church may have the spirit of the world. Our religion may be selfish, seeking our own salvation and happiness alone. Or our religion may be, in a stricter sense, worldly, seeking to have with it just as much as we can of its enjoyments and possessions as possible. Or the worldliness may manifest itself in the modes of thought and action, in the principles and practices which are of the wisdom of this world, being allowed to rule and to guide in the work of Christ and the worship of God. Whatever is not of the love of God and of the Spirit of Christ is of the world and its spirit.

But it is the Spirit alone who can convince of this sin. He is able to lead each believer to see the world not only in others, but in himself, possibly in forms of worldliness or worldly conformity he had never suspected. He is able to open our eyes, in the meekness of wisdom and the humility of love, to the state of our own congregation or church, or to the state of the church as a whole. We need both. Nehemiah and Daniel and the saints of old confessed their own sins and the sins of the people. Let us plead with our lord Jesus, out of whose mouth goes the sharp two-edged sword, to speak his searching word. 'Not of the world', so as to make it go through our whole heart and being. It is one of the root words in the revelation of himself, in his discovery to his disciples of their likeness to himself, in his intercession with the Father: it must be one of the key-words in any true revival, in all true prayer and preparation for it. Let us plead with him to speak it in power until each of us and all his church has heard it.

Every heresy, every neglect or denial of God's truth, weakens the spiritual life. The rejection of the faith in the divinity of Christ, of the atonement through blood, or justification by faith, or regeneration by the Spirit, endangers the life of the church. But of all heresies the worst, the heresy of heresies is a worldly spirit. It dispossesses the Spirit of God and makes every truth powerless. It brings the church into subjection to the god of this world. If there is one prayer we need it is this: Lord, show us what thou meanest: Not of the world! As we see what it is to have a supernatural life and calling, and what a shame to sacrifice this to a worldly spirit, and are able to judge how far this is done in the church, our whole heart will cry out for revival as the one only thing that can help the church.

One word more. Let us believe that deliverance from a worldly spirit is possible. Christ promised it: 'Be of good cheer, I have overcome the world.' John testified of it: 'Whatsoever is born of God overcometh the world.' The new life, the life of the Holy Spirit, can overcome the spirit of the world. Let but God's children set their hearts upon, and cry to God for, deliverance from the bondage of this subjection to the world that crucified their lord. He will give it. They may not know all that is implied in the word world, there may be differences in defining it – let them but give themselves up, in the willingness to let go, and be entirely made free from what God counts 'of the world', to the teaching and filling of that Spirit of God who can dispossess the spirit of the world. God is gracious, God is faithful, God is mighty. And as the answer to prayer comes to ourselves, we shall have true courage to pray for our brethren.

Chapter 5

The Spirit of God Revealing the Things of God

> *'Who among men knoweth the things of a man, save the spirit of the man, which is in him? Even so the things of God none knoweth, save the Spirit of God. But we received, not the spirit of the world, but the spirit which is of God; that we might know the things that are freely given to us by God.'*
> 1 Corinthians 2: 11–12

In the Epistle to the Romans, people who gave law a place in the world it never had before, and whose influence still rules in our modern world, Paul preached the Gospel in its relation to law. The Gospel was a revelation of the righteousness of God, and revealed the way in which he himself was righteous, and could righteously accept the ungodly as righteous too. The Corinthians were a people with whom wisdom was everything. In the epistle to them Paul shows that just as absolute as was the need and provision of divine righteousness was the need and provision of divine wisdom. As no man knoweth the things of God save the Spirit of God, so we receive the Spirit of God so that we may know the things that are freely given us of God. In Romans we learn *what* the Gospel that is to be preached; in Corinthians *how* it is to be preached. The church of the Reformation owes everything to the truth of a divine righteousness. They have, alas, not been equally jealous of the doctrine of a divine wisdom as man's only hope for knowing the things of God. The preaching of the utter insufficiency of man's righteousness has not been accompanied, as it should have been, by the preaching of the utter insufficiency of his wisdom. The consequences have been most disastrous. And nothing has suffered more from it than just the doctrine of the divine righteousness. Too often preached not in the power of the Holy Spirit but of human wisdom, it has not been the power of God unto salvation, or had not led the believer into the close and full fellowship with God it was meant to. The restoration of the truth of the teaching of the Holy Spirit being as indispensable as the forgiveness through Christ's blood would indeed bring us a Second Reformation, a New Pentecost.

After speaking in the previous chapter about the wisdom of man, it is right our first subject should be the Holy Spirit as the revealer of the things of God. For more than one reason. It will show us at the very outset how the great evil we have spoken of can be cured, as we see how sure and sufficient the provision God has made is. It will so help us to test the preaching and the life around us by the standard of Scripture. It will give point and force to our prayer when we are asked by Christ, as he always does ask: 'What wilt thou that I do unto thee?'

We shall know what to look out for and expect, in answer to our prayer. We shall learn to claim for ourselves the full revival blessing – a life daily and wholly under the teaching of the Spirit. And so, even in the reading of this book, we shall be kept from trusting to impressions however deep, or convictions however strong, and at each step ask the Spirit of God to reveal to us the things of God. So will our prayer be that the actual beginning of the coming revival. With a stroke of a pen Paul reveals to us in one simple sentence the necessity of the teaching of the Spirit of God: 'No man knoweth the things of a man, save the spirit of a man which is in him, even so the things of God none knoweth, save the Spirit of God.' No one can know what goes on in the heart of a man but the man himself. How much more, as we think of God as an infinite, holy, spiritual and incomprehensible being – how much more must it be true, 'the things of God none knoweth save the Spirit of God, and he to whom the Spirit reveals them'? He is the very life of God. He searches the deep things of God, because God is a Spirit, it is by the Spirit that God is what he is; he alone can reveal the things of God. In one sense Christ revealed the Father. But that revelation was only an objective one. With all that Christ taught his disciples their apprehensions of divine things were dark and ineffective. Christ promised them that the Holy Spirit should come to show them all things he had taught, and all that there was in him. The reason the Spirit could do this was that as he was the inmost life in God, he could enter into their inmost life, and communicate there, the actual participation of the things of God in their living power and blessedness. Thoughts and reasoning only give knowledge in the mind about a thing, while they do not give the heart the actual experience and blessedness of what they represent. True knowledge, whether of earthly or heavenly things, is always life and experience and possession. Reason can give us abundant knowledge about God; it can give us nothing of God himself or that knowledge of him which is life eternal. The Spirit is the very life and power of God; all that he reveals is truth and power. He gives us to know God because he enters into the life and communicates the very thing which the word speaks in spirit and in truth. Through him we know God by what he is and gives and works in us. Thoughts can only give pictures of spiritual things. At times these may be beautiful and delightful pictures, that make most pleasing impressions. They may waken strong desires in the heart and stir the will to its utmost effort, but they never can give or reveal the life. This is the sole prerogative of the Spirit of God.

He can do this not only because he is the Spirit of God, but because he can and does enter into the very spirit of man. The spirit of man was breathed into him by God; we are his offspring. As the Spirit of God, the Creator, he has the mysterious power of entering and inhabiting the spirit of man. As the Spirit of God, the Redeemer, he has given us a new spirit, within which he dwells and acts, secretly inspiring it with all the life and graces of the Lord Jesus. This is the reason why Paul says in the words following our text, that the things of God are spiritually discerned and that only spiritual Christians can profit by spiritual teaching; as long as there are worldly disposition and conduct they cannot bear it (see 1 Cor. 2:14; 3:1, 3). The Spirit so communicates the divine life, that not only is the natural, unconverted man incapable of receiving this, but even the converted man, as long as he yields to the flesh, with sins like jealousy and strife, cannot apprehend this. It needs a spiritual ear and eye, opened by God's Spirit, a spiritual nature longing to know more of God, his love, his will. The Holy Spirit has been given to all, but only those I have just described are really taught by him. Only they can say in experience, 'we have received, not the spirit of the world, but the Spirit which is of God, that we might know the things which are freely given us of God.'

The teaching office of the Holy Spirit is inseparable from the other two, his sanctifying and strengthening work. They all go together. He teaches to sanctify, he teaches by sanctifying, and so fitting the holy heart to receive his spiritual instruction. His teaching is strengthening; it is always accompanied by a divine enabling to act out, what he has revealed. One or other of the three may at times, or for a time, in different members of the body, be more prominent. He is ever the one Spirit in whom they are altogether, and who, whatever part of his work may stand out more distinctly in our consciousness, works in us as the Spirit of truth, the Spirit of holiness, the Spirit of power. He is all this because he is the Spirit of life by whom we truly live a divine life.

This work of the Spirit is now the great mark of the New Testament church, of true Christianity. The seal or heavenly stamp God has set upon every believer and upon his church is the Holy Spirit, who knows the things of God, given into the heart to make them know these. It is not enough that a child be born of healthy real parents, his future depends greatly upon the teacher to whom he is entrusted and the education he received. With the child of God everything depends upon his knowing, submitting to, waiting on, and carrying out the teaching of the Holy Spirit. The feebleness of the church stems from this being not known and believed and acted on. A revival in the church will mean nothing less than this, that ministers and members will together be led to give the Holy Spirit, the divine and only teacher, the place God wants him to take.

Let us just think what the faith and the experience of the blessing this truth brings us would mean in the Christian life. Just consider the influence a full appreciation of it would have on a believer who seeks to give God the whole tithe, his whole heart and life. He begins to know, not in thought but in faith and power, that the Spirit of God is in him. Not as something alongside and additional to his own life, partly and occasionally influencing it, but as the inmost life of our very selves, not only controlling or helping but far more, as the moving spring and power of our being, inspiring and impelling us in all we are and do. He begins to see what he needs. First of all to have a deeper sense of his own spiritual ignorance, of the utter impotence and the great danger of all the mere mind-knowledge with its beautiful images and impressions. Then to bow in great stillness of soul before God, renouncing his own wisdom as utterly as his own righteousness, and to ask that the consciousness of the divine indwelling of the Spirit may be given by the Father himself. He learns that in every act of prayer or communion with God's Word, in every desire or resolve in connection with divine things, his first duty is to wait in humble dependence upon God, to have the activity of nature restrained and mortified, and the heart trained into the habit of faith that the Spirit will teach and work. As he gradually realises that the Holy Spirit is indeed within him, he bows with a deeper reverence and fear, but also with a fuller dependence and assurance before the Father who gives the Spirit. And he learns what at first he did not understand, that so far from the Spirit being a power in us that we can use or call up, his presence makes us more absolutely and necessarily dependent on the Father. Just as our Lord, who had received the Spirit without measure, did not dare to speak a word or do a work without the Father giving it him each moment, so the true faith of the Spirit's indwelling bends us in the most absolute weakness to the footstool of God's throne. When God made man, it was that he might live in man, imparting by his personal presence all the goodness he was capable of, and working himself in his will and affections what man was to do and to be. Pentecost restored what Paradise lost. The believer yields himself trustfully to what God would have him be, because he now knows that the Spirit, who knows the things of God, reveals and works in him the things that are freely given us of God.

To understand aright what this teaching of the Spirit is, there are three things we must specially remember. The first, that it is all from within. It is by influencing, by renewing, by purifying the life, that the Spirit gives the experimental knowledge of God's truth. Out of the light of life, wrought within our feeling and willing and acting, spiritual wisdom and understanding is born. The second, that this power and energy of the Spirit is given on one condition – that of entire possession. As a teacher cannot teach unless he has the undivided attention of his pupil, the Holy Spirit demands the entire control of the life. A great deal of prayer for the teaching or the filling of the Spirit is vain, because the seeker is not faithful in obedience to that measure of the Spirit which he already has. The Spirit claims our whole being. And the third essential element in the teaching is that it is only communicated and to be received by faith. The movings of the Spirit cannot be known or felt until we begin to act. It is when, while feeling our weakness, we believe in the hidden presence and power within us and begin to act, that his guidance and strength are known. Faith in his indwelling and most certain leading, much faith in the Father who works by the Spirit, unceasing faith in the Lord Jesus, in union with whom we have the Spirit flowing through us – this faith will receive the fullness of the Spirit. This is the revival we must seek for, the restoration of the Holy Spirit to his place as the inward teacher, having complete possession and control of heart and life.

What a change it would make in a church if there were a number of men and women given over to be thus taught and led by the Spirit of God. And what a change in our meetings for worship or for work, in our churches or our assemblies and councils, if men and women regarded it as the most prominent characteristic of their relationships with each other that the Spirit of God had taught and was teaching them, hour by hour, the things of God. And what a still greater change when it was known that a majority of our ministers were Spirit-taught men who could say, God hath revealed it to us by his Spirit, which things we speak not in word which man's wisdom teacheth, but which the Spirit teacheth, combining spiritual things with spiritual. And what a joy if the churches were waking up, and that in our colleges and institutions for training ministers the first object was now to help men to become true ministers of the New Covenant, ministers of the Spirit, men and women who lived their own life as taught by the Spirit in the things of God, and were therefore able to lead others into the truly spiritual life. Yes, what a change it would be.

With man it is impossible! But with God all things are possible! Oh, let us pray in faith for a revived church and a revived ministry. If there is one thing sure, it is that the Father giveth the Holy Spirit to them that ask him. You cannot doubt this. If there is one thing for which Christ is elevated on the throne for, it is that he may baptise with the Holy Spirit, and give streams of living water from everyone who believes in him. You dare not doubt this. If there is one thing God meant his church to be filled with, it is, oh listen, it is the Holy Spirit. And shall we then fear and be unbelieving? God forbid! We may, we will believe that God, in answer to the prayers of his people, will work a mighty change.

Chapter 6

Judgment Beginning at the House of God

'Go through the city and smite: Slay utterly old and young ... and begin at my sanctuary.'
Ezekiel 9:5–6

'The time is come that judgment must begin at the house of God.' 1 Peter 4:17

Peter had evidently read and pondered the passage in Ezekiel of which the words: 'begin at my sanctuary' are the centre. He had noticed how, before the awful judgments the prophet had to announce against the nations that had oppressed Israel (Chapters 25–32), the force of God's anger had, in the first part of the book, been revealed against his own people. Peter had learnt the great law that the holiness of God always seeks first to deal with sin in his own house and church. It is only as we know and submit to this that we can rightly apprehend the fearfulness and the certainty of his judgments on them that obey not the Gospel of God. The power to feel and preach the wrath coming upon the disobedient and salvation from it will depend greatly on our insight into what it means that God begins at the sanctuary, on the experience in our own heart of God having dealt in judgment with the sins of our Christian life.

It is well known that the keyword of the prophet Ezekiel, occurring more than sixty times, is this, 'Ye shall know that I am the Lord.' To know God is eternal life. It is the privilege, the joy, the strength of his people. God can bestow no higher favour than to make himself known. When his glory, his holiness, his power, his nearness, his saving love, are revealed in the soul, it has all.

Since sin entered into the world the two great attributes which we need to know by experience if we are to know God are the two which are united in his holiness, his righteousness and his love. In Ezekiel we find that it is in the revelation of these two that God is to be known. On the one side you have God made known in judgment in passages like these in chapter 5: 'I will judge thee according to thy ways, and ye shall know that I am the Lord.' 'I will recompense thee according to thy ways, and ye shall know that I am the Lord that smiteth.' 'According to their desire will I judge them, and they shall know that I am the Lord' (5:4, 9, 27). So later, 'Ye shall know that I am the Lord when I set my face against them. Ye shall bear the sins of your idols, and ye shall know that I am the Lord.' And then on the other hand, God made known in mercy: 'Ye shall know that I am the Lord when I shall bring you into the land, when I have wrought with you for my name's sake. I will raise up for them a plant of renown, thus shall they know that I the Lord their God am with them ... The heathen shall know that I am the Lord, when I shall be sanctified in you before their eyes (36:23; 37:28).

'I will put my Spirit in you and ye shall live, then shall ye know that the Lord hath spoken it and performed it.'

And thus it ever is. The revelation of God, the true living knowledge of God in a world of sin can only come through the judgment on sin that brings deliverance from sin. Revival among God's people can only come as we yield to him to judge sin in us. As we wait on him in the way of his judgments we shall learn to sing of judgment and mercy.

After God's declaration in chapter 7 that he would judge his people, he takes the prophet in chapter 8, 'in the visions of God', to see all the wicked abominations that were being done in the house of God in Jerusalem. While the men who committed them said 'The Lord seeth us not', God saw, and felt, and was angry. And so in chapter 9 the prophet hears the command given, after a mark has been set on the forehead of the few who sigh and cry for the abominations that were being done, to six men, each with his weapon in his hand, to go through the city and smite, and slay utterly without mercy old and young. And then the word came in: 'And begin at my sanctuary.' And then follows: 'Then they began at the ancient men which were before the house.' The higher the privilege the greater the sin. The nearer to God's holiness and its judgment. The more God loves us as his people, the more jealous is he of our sins. From the very nature of things, from the very nature of God, and of our relation to him, it cannot be otherwise. Judgment must begin at the house of God. God's people must be subject to it, must yield themselves to it, if they are to be witnesses to the world of God's saving power, if through them the Holy Spirit is to convict the world of sin. Let us endeavour to take in the lessons that our subject suggests in connection with the prayer for the revival of God's people.

1. There may be sin in God's sanctuary that men think or know little of. The prophet was shown by God what the men did 'in the dark, every man in the chambers of his imagining.' They still clung to God's house, they called it the temple of Jehovah; they were ready to die for it as the centre and the symbol of their national relig-

ion, and yet they defiled it with their abominations. And they never dreamt how near and how terrible God's judgment on them would be.

May it not be thus with the church of our day? May it not be that the formality, and the lukewarmness and worldliness, the self-seeking and pleasure-seeking, which marks the great majority of our professing Christians, are being looked upon by God as 'wicked abominations' in his house, while we have very little conception of their evil? God led Ezekiel from the outer to the inner court. May it not be that the sins that are found in the hearts and lives of the more earnest and inner circle among Christians, the lack of humility and love, the trust in human wisdom and human support, the neglect of the continual leading of the Spirit and the full imitation of Christ, may it not be that these things are displeasing and grieving God to an extent that we have no conception of? Let us ask carefully whether there be not in the church, or in our own heart, much that makes it most needful that judgment begin at the house of God.

2. If the church is to be an habitation of God in the Spirit, if God is really to dwell among his people, sin must be judged and cast out. Judgment must begin at the sanctuary. In the whole universe of things *sin* is the only thing that can hide God or hinder his being to his people what he is in his nature, a very fountain of love, goodness and happiness. The whole history of Israel proves to us that God delights in and blessed obedience – that he turns away from sin. It is just as true in the experience of the saints today. Any deeper experience of God's presence to save from sin and to reveal his nearness is usually preceded by a new discovery of sin and a more complete deliverance from it. The failure of so much earnest sighing and struggling to attain a deeper and more settled peace and victory is almost always due to not allowing God himself to deal with the sin that is overcoming us. Any revival of holiness and devotion to Christ's service will be but partial and passing until believers are brought to see that the ordinary sins of daily life are no

longer tolerated and the power of Christ to cast them out is known and claimed. The whole of the book of Ezekiel proves how God's being known in judgment was the one condition of his being known in salvation. The first twenty-five chapters with his judgments on his people, the next ten with his judgments on their enemies, are the introductions to the wonderful blessings that are promised in chapter 36, and following. All is gathered up in the wonderful promises: 'The heathen shall know that I am the Lord when I shall be sanctified in you before their eyes ... And the heathen shall know that I the Lord do sanctify Israel, when my sanctuary shall be in the midst of them for evermore' (36:23; 37:28). It is when God's judgments on his people have sanctified them, and the sanctuary of God, his holy presence is seen among them, that there will be power to convince the world, and the nations shall know that he is Lord.

3. To discover sin is God's work. 'The hand of the Lord fell upon me', 'the Spirit lifted me up, and brought me in the visions of God to Jerusalem' – it was thus the prophet was led to see what many people living in Jerusalem never knew. It is this we need in our assemblies – the hand of God falling on us, and making us feel that he is dealing with us; the Spirit lifting us between earth and heaven, above the things of earth, and bringing us in the visions of God to Jerusalem. Yes, let us plead for this in our assemblies, or in secret – the hand, and the Spirit, and the visions of God to bring us to see what is the real state of God's church as he sees it. In plain words, let us beseech God to show us, in the visions of God, what he thinks of the state of his people, of our own state. It is so easy to congratulate each other on all the signs of advance we see, as compared with the past, that we have lost the power of realising how much evil and sin there is, as compared with God's standard. The good is often the greatest enemy of the best. People rest satisfied with a lesser good, with what was meant to be but a beginning of something far higher and better, and never think of seeking God's best, the full and over-

flowing measure he has promised. Let us ask him to show everything in the life of his people, or our own, that he condemns and grieves over, that he would have different. Until we see hidden evil, the abominable things concerning which he has a controversy and for which he withholds the blessing, we shall never desire his work of judgment or his way of blessing, nor yield to his command, 'Begin at my sanctuary.'

4. God himself must judge the sin. He alone can do it. This is often the cause of lifelong failure with believers, that when they see sin they seek to deal with it themselves. And by dealing with it they have failed to conquer, they count it a permanent thing that it cannot be overcome. Oh, Christians, let *God* deal with your sin. The expression is found in the prophet Ezekiel: 'Can thine heart endure, or can thine hands be strong, in the days that I shall deal with thee? I the Lord have spoken it, and I will do it' (Ezek. 22:14). If you would have your heart broken down, and your hands made utterly weak, so you no longer resist God, let God deal with your sin. Bring the sin that is discovered in his temple, in your body, or in your heart, to him, and let him execute his fierce judgment on it. Be it the lust of the flesh, sin in the body and its appetites; be it the lust of the eye, sin in choosing the visible above the invisible; be it the pride of life, sin in preferring self before God or the neighbour – bring it out before a holy God, give it into his charge, and ask him to deal with it, to execute judgment on it. Ask him to do what he has spoken, not to spare and not to pity, but to pour out his fury upon it, till the sinful deed is utterly destroyed before his presence. 'They shall know that I am the Lord when I lay my vengeance on them.' Give your sins over to God's vengeance, wait on him as the God of judgment, then will he fulfil the promise, 'From all your filthiness and from all your idols will I cleanse you.'

In connection with the subject of this volume – The Coming Revival – all that has been said leads up to two thoughts on which I cannot insist too earnestly. Begin at my sanctuary. The word calls us to listen as God tells us that the feebleness and the failure of so much work for him is owing to the state of his church – his temple has been defiled. Until God's people are put right we cannot possibly expect any great change in the world or any increased power or blessing. In all questions about the causes of failure, about new and better methods of work, about preparation for revival, about conditions of prayer that will certainly be answered, there sounds from heaven the voice of God: Begin at my sanctuary. We must set our heart upon the state of God's people and on what is to be done to bring them where God would have them.

The other thought is: If God's church is to be roused, if believers are to be led to a life of greater devotion to Jesus and his service; if streams of living water are to flow out of them; if the interests of Christ's kingdom and the salvation of souls are to become their first object in life and their enthusiasm, as God wants them to be, the work must begin in them allowing God to deal with the sin of the personal life. It is in his sanctuary, his holy place alone that God can be known in his holiness. It is in his temple in our body, in his home in our heart, that his power must be personally known to deliver from sin, if we are in true faith and devotion to live for others. Begin at my sanctuary. Let the temple that has been defiled be cleansed. Let the heart sins be dealt with by God. And the word shall be fulfilled: 'Then will I magnify myself and sanctify myself and I will be known in the eyes of many nations; and they shall know that I am the Lord.'

Chapter 7

A Missionary Revival

*'Ye shall receive power when the Holy Ghost
is come upon you: and ye shall be my
witnesses, both in Jerusalem and in all Judaea
and Samaria and unto the uttermost part of
the earth.'* Acts 1:8

Here we have the object and the condition of the pentecostal blessing of the Holy Spirit. The object was not merely, as is often said, the birth of the Christian church, but its equipment for the service of witnessing for Christ unto the uttermost ends of the earth. The condition was the willingness to receive it for this purpose, the readiness to go to the ends of the earth. The love of God is world-wide and universal. 'God so loved the world that he gave his only begotten son, that whosoever believeth in him should have eternal life.' 'Who willeth that all men should be saved.' 'Not willing that any should perish, but that all should come to repentance.' On the cross Christ died for all. 'He is a propitiation not for our sins only, but also for the whole world.' At the foot of the throne he gave the charge, 'Go into all the world and preach the gospel to every creature.' And so the promise of the Holy Spirit in his pentecostal fullness of power comes for the one purpose of bringing the life of the church as a whole, and each believer, into harmony with the will of the Father and the work of the Son, so that they only live for what God and Christ live for, the glory of God in the salvation of men amd women. The eternal Spirit, through whom Christ gave himself a sacrifice to God for all, is the Spirit who now dwells in us. He has come to glorify Christ, to carry on his work of glorifying the Father in and through us. The Spirit is come to fill us with the love and zeal and strength that will make us live and die that every creature may know the love of God. As we give ourselves to this and wait at God's feet for his orders, the power of the Holy Spirit will come upon us.

We are praying for a revival. We are praying for a mighty renewing of God's Holy Spirit. Are we really preaching to God's people that the one object that lies nearest God's heart, and for which he is willing to give the Spirit in power, is to enable every child of his to live wholly and undividedly for his glory and the kingdom of his Son? Are we preaching that the one condition on which we may expect a mighty revival, making God's people new, is the readiness to give themselves up to the possession of the Holy Spirit, to use as he will to witness for Christ in a world that knows him not? This witnessing will begin at Jerusalem, at home; it will enlarge the heart and not rest till it has reached every creature. A missionary revival can only be part of a larger revival – the restoration of believers to a life of true spiritual exclusive devotion to Christ and his service. A true spiritual revival in the Christian life will be the power of the missionary revival.

I have often been very much impressed with the solemn, the honourable, the exceeding blessed privilege belonging to the directors and committee of our missionary societies. Now again in reading, with intense interest and continual thanksgiving, the history of the Church Missionary Society, I have felt what it meant that they are not only the link between the church and the heathen, receiving on the one hand the men and women and the money needed for the work, and disposing of them on the other as appears best. They are much more. They are the link between Christ and his church for the carrying out of his last command. It is they more than others who realise the slowness of the church to give the men and women the Lord claims, with the lack of interest and prayer and liberality that so much prevails. It is they who specially have to strive to stir up interest, to circulate information, to organise systematic and united effort. It is they who are brought face to face with the great question, what is, at root, the cause of the lack of zeal for Christ's glory and the salvation of souls? And how is the evil to be cured? What must be done to give effect to our arguments and appeals? And to make the sacrifice of all we have, to him who redeemed us and them, that it may be used in giving him the travail of his soul and the glory due to his name, the natural, spontaneous, joyful expression of a life delighting in him and his service?

Of all the questions our missionary directors have to face there are none more important or difficult than these. In my student days in Holland I heard an address from the gifted Professor Beets: *What the church owes the heathen*. A year later he gave a second one: *How the heathen repays the church*. He spoke of all the blessing that returns to the church in many ways, and specially in the quickening of its spiritual life. As this is seen it will be felt that this is hardly secondary to the great work of sending the Gospel to the perishing as is the work committed to the leaders of our societies to take the highest ground in their appeal for support, and enforce on every Christian the urgent need, the absolute duty, the unspeakable blessedness, and the actual possibility of giving every breath and every power to the Lord who bought us with his blood. A life of consecration to Christ, a life of continual thought and love and prayer for Christ's kingdom, will then not be regarded as the duty or the privilege of a few, but as the will of God for each of his children, the only true conformity to Christ, the only real blessedness on earth. If there is to be any true revival, we must be ready to make it the revival of a full missionary consecration. If there is to be a true revival it must be the revival of a deep, a true spiritual life. From this point of view let us study the missionary revival we wish to pray for.

Think of its infinite importance. Look at God's world fallen away from him, under the power of the evil one, who is now the god of this world. Look at all those thousand million heathens and Muslims, who have never learnt that the Son of God came from heaven to be their Saviour. On each one God's love is resting. For each one Christ's blood avails and pleads. To bring the Gospel to each one the Holy Spirit has been given. The church has been taken by Christ into partnership in his great work of conquering the world for God. She has failed terribly in her duty. All the pleadings of God's servants during the last hundred years – how little results they have brought. And is not this the one thing under the sun that is of more consequence than any other? In the history of states and individuals there are thousands of things of exceeding interest and importance. But does not this exceed and overpower all – that God shall have the world back again – that his glory as God shall be given him by every creature – that a perishing world shall know the salvation of God? Again I say, the glory of God and the salvation of millions depends on this, that the church wakes up to her duty. Nothing can exceed the importance of a great missionary revival.

Think of its urgent need. Nothing less will avail. Sermons and meetings, addresses and appeals, organisation and effort – these all have their value and effect, but they are not sufficient, something more is needed. We need to realise the power of the flesh and the world, as seen in a selfish and worldly religion. The incapacity to grasp spiritually the meaning of God's command and his promise of the power of the Holy Spirit for our work, can only be cast out by a special intervention of God's omnipotence. That there is some mighty power holding down Christians many testify. Just listen to the witness of Mr Coillard, after he had spent two years in visiting the churches of France and Switzerland, England and Scotland. He had to an extent that exceeded the expectations of many, obtained men and money for his work. He had enjoyed fellowship with many of God's saints, and praised God for much that he saw. And yet he gives his general impression of the lives of Christians in these words: 'It is high time for the church to bestir herself; we have played at missions long enough. What we need is to cast aside the mask of all mere religiosity, all that is simply form and tradition, and to live at the height of our profession. Long enough have we patronised the work of God and interested ourselves in it as amateurs; what we want today is to make it our work, to feel each of us his personal responsibility, to spend and be spent for it – not what we possess and can spare, but our very selves.

'When we see missionary meetings so run after – when we hear these stirring hymns, these sublime and stirring protestations of our compassion for the perishing heathen, and our entire devotion to him whom we acknowledge as king, should we not expect to see a whole crusade on the march for the conquest of the world? One might suppose that all we have and all we hope for had been laid on the altar, waiting for nothing but the fire of heaven.

'And in reality, what have we done? What have we given? What have we sacrificed? Where does this spirit show itself in the details of daily life? What discipline are we willing to submit to? What ease, what luxuries, have we denied ourselves?' The need for a missionary revival is urgent.

Think of its character. What must be the nature of a true missionary revival? An increased missionary

interest, awakened by intelligence from the field, and
stirring appeals, is not enough. It is simply temporary,
passing away after a time. We need a devotion and an
enthusiasm having its root, its strength, and its perma-
nence through all surrounding changes, in a personal
devotion to Christ Jesus, in a life rooted in Christ. In *The
History of the Church Missionary Society* we read (2:34):

'At a time when new missionaries were urgently
needed, and the CMS Committee were asking for special prayer that they might be raised up, Ridgeway
reminded the Society that what was needed was really
another Pentecost. The lack of missionaries is, no doubt,
the point of immediate pressure. But that can be met
only by increased effectiveness on the part of the whole
spiritual body, in more single dedication to the Lord's
work, more holy energy, more true devotion. And how
shall this be, except by a new effusion of that Spirit, who
is the mover and promoter to all holy action, and the dispenser of all needful gifts and grace?'

In the closing pages of his *Short History* the author
says, after speaking of the cause of praise we have in all
that God had wrought: 'In the face of the appalling fact
that one-half of the globe has never heard of Christ, how
can we speak of "the great Society" and "its colossal
increase"? The real truth is that our present efforts are,
on the part of the church as a whole, almost like playing
at missions. A great revolution has to take place in
Christian public opinion if the church of Christ is really
to do the work committed to her by the Lord.' (p. 173.)
Yes, nothing else is needed than a revolution. And this
will be effected by nothing but that power of the Holy
Spirit which can restore the health of the whole body
with all its members that the work for God's kingdom
shall be its joy and crown, as naturally as it is the fruit
that is born by the healthy tree.

Think of its certain prospect. There is no symptom of
a feeble and diseased life more terrible than that we get
so accustomed to it as not to believe any great change
possible. We settle down and rest content with what we

are; we find reason for regarding our state as the best possible one on earth. Do let us fix our heart upon the purpose and the power and the promise of God until we begin to see him, who worketh all things according to the purpose of his will, just waiting to be gracious and to give his Holy Spirit to them that ask him. God's heart is set on the salvation of men and women; the gift of his Son and Spirit is the proof of it. God's heart is set upon making us fellow-labourers, sharers in the glory and blessedness of his work. For every command the promise holds good; My grace is sufficient for thee. To the last great command, 'every creature', obedience is possible. The promise of the Spirit is unchangeably linked with it. Do let us believe: a missionary revival is possible. God is able. God longs so to transform the hearts of his children, that the kingdom of Christ shall be the absorbing passion of their lives. He will do it for those who cry to him for it. As he does this others will be wakened and blessed too. And instead of, as in most revivals, the conversion of sinners only bringing a temporary warmth and rousing, without leading them into the life of full consecration, the revival that begins with God's children, and aims at nothing less than leading them each to make the extension of the kingdom the one object and joy of their existence, will soon overflow on the unsaved at home and abroad, and their new birth will bring them into an atmosphere of health and service in the power of the Spirit. Such has been too little the result of the ordinary revival.

Such a revival is possible. 'The things that are impossible with men and women are possible with God.' Of such a revival there is a certain prospect if God's people are ready to seek and welcome it. The Father's promise, the promise our King gave when ascending the throne, the promise of Pentecost means nothing less: 'Ye shall receive the power of the Holy Spirit coming on you, and be my witnesses to the uttermost parts of the earth.' Nothing less than this is the church's heritage if she will but claim it.

Shall we not pray as never before for a revival in the life of God's people that shall fit them to fulfil their duty to God and the world, that shall make missionary effort in very deed the supreme end, the chief glory of the church? If there is anything more needed to urge us to such prayer, let it be this. The proverb says: As the mother, so the daughter. The complaint in missionary churches of the weakness of many of our converts is most natural when we look at the general tone of our Christians at home. The influence of the revival of believers in the older churches on missionaries and converts abroad will be certain and most blessed. The power of the Spirit of God in the mother churches wakening to a higher devotion will infallibly affect all their branches in heathen lands. We cannot impart to them more than we have. Shall we not beseech God that what we give them shall indeed be streams of living water in all their divine purity and abundance and quickening power as they flow from under the throne of God and the Lamb?

Chapter 8

God so Loved the World

'God so loved the world, that he gave his only begotten Son, that whosoever believeth in him should not perish, but have everlasting life.'
John 3:16

The word 'whosoever' has generally been considered the key to this wonderful text. To thousands that word has given the courage to say – 'whosoever': that includes me – the love, and the Son and the life – they are all for me. And many an earnest worker has, in pleading with or for the most helpless case, found his strength in the confidence – 'whosoever', cannot mean anything but everyone. There is not one excluded; to each one I dare to say the love, and the Son, and the life, are for thee.

This is the individual aspect of the word. But just this includes a wider one, its universal aspect. It says of every child of man who belongs to this world, that the love and the life are for him. And the word calls us, who say we believe it, not only faith to us to use it with every soul whom we meet needing help, but to allow it to exert its full force on us in all its divine largeness, as it proclaims the right every crature has to the love and life of God's Son. Not till every thought of that love is linked in our heart inseparably with the blessed truth: that love belongs to all, do we really begin to understand it. As we wait for the Holy Spirit to reveal in us how that love longs to get possession of all, for whom it was meant, we shall find in that 'whatsoever' a mighty plea for a life wholly giving itself up to be filled with that love, and to find its only joy and glory in living for what God lives for – to love and save the world.

Yes, we have too exclusively used this word in its application to individuals, as a plea for them to come and accept Christ and eternal life. God meant that, in its fullness of meaning, it should be a plea with his redeemed ones, who do indeed see its meaning and believe its truth, to look upon every fellow-creature as one of this whosoever multitude, and not to rest till each one knows the love in which they have a share.

This thought leads us up to some of the great mysteries of redemption. There is the partnership in the revelation of God's love into which Christ has taken up his people; his having made himself dependent upon them for the continuation and completion of his work; and – greatest mystery of all – their terrible unfaithfulness to this their holy calling. Near nineteen centuries have elapsed since he spoke the glorious word combining precept and privilege: the Gospel to every creature. And, still, two-thirds of the human race have never heard of him. And of the remaining third more than half live in ignorance of the wonderful love and life he revealed to us, that we might impart it to others, might bring it to all. From God's heaven that 'whosoever', like the sun in its unlimited and unstinted glory, shines down on every soul dying in darkness. To us is given the honour, as those to whom the love has been committed, who live in the enjoyment of its power and blessing, of having fellowship with him who spake the great 'whosoever', and, like him, of living and dying to make it known. And the most of us have been content to accept the word for ourselves, and to confine the love to our own selfish hearts. And the best of us have yearned and pleaded and sacrificed, that we might know nothing but this love, that our heart and life might ever be overflowing with it for others to drink.

If a revival is to come, greater, deeper, broader than any that has yet been, one great part of its power will be in the conviction it will bring of the sin and shame of all the carnal ease, and comfort, and self-indulgence in which we have been living, while the dying, perishing world which has been given into our charge was waiting for us, and the infinite love that had entrusted itself to us, was mourning that we were so slow to go and tell of it. The conviction of sin must be greater, deeper, broader, than we have known it. Judgment will have to begin at the house of God. The great deep will have to be broken up. The formality and worldliness, the selfishness and self-confidence and self-complacency of much of our religion will have to be revealed in the light of the actual life, and worship, and devotion, and self-sacrifice in the power of the Spirit to which God has called us. Above all, the sin of having had the love of God to the world given into our heart for the one purpose of communicating it, and then having congratulated ourselves on the small gifts of silver or gold for which we sought to commute our personal service, will become to us such a burning thing, that our penitent confession and our cry for pardon and deliverance will work an entire revolution. We shall indeed yield ourselves and wait for the Holy Spirit to work the life of Christ Jesus in us, that, even as he, each of us in our measure may live exclusively for the glory of God in the salvation of souls.

The sin of this neglect in the church of God, in not accepting and proclaiming this great 'whosoever' of God's love, in not living to make God's love known has had and is having such appalling consequences, that even Christians fail to realise what is meant. We are told that there are thirty million heathens every year passing away into utter darkness. We count up the years, and think how this has been going on through the ages since Christ gave the great command to his church as its watchword. The mind refuses to take it. It is as if this wonderful love of God might have interfered, might have done more. It looks as if it is too awful to put upon the church, upon us the Christians of today too, the burden and the guilt of these perishing multitudes. And yet it is so. The eternal love gave the Son to reveal it on earth. The Son committed it to his disciples, to his body, the church, with a charge as plain as words can make it, to carry that love to every creature, to all nations, to the ends of the earth. That was the one thing the church was sent for into the world, even as he had been sent, and for nothing else. It is due to nothing but selfishness, and unfaithfulness, and neglect on the part of the church, that this holy mission has not been so badly accomplished. More than one person has said: We have been playing at missions. And yet how we congratulate ourselves on all the wakened missionary interest. And all the while the number of believers who really follow in the footsteps of Christ, and count it their joy to give their whole heart and strength, to live and die, whether it be in prayer or work, for the glory of God in the salvation of souls, is so small.

Nothing can effect a change in this but a revival of a type we have not yet known. A revival that will, by the divine power of the Holy Spirit, open the eyes of believers to see how very wrong and low their conceptions have been of the life that God actually wants them to live. A revival that will make the last command of Christ live in the heart of every true disciple. A revival that will shake and lift our churches, and separate to an unselfish and unworldly life all who are willing to live wholly for God. A revival that will bind together the whole church in an enthusiasm for Christ and his kingdom. A revival in which the true following and imitation of Christ, in his living exclusively to bring the love of God to perishing men, will be the mark of the normal Christian life.

The question will be asked, and it is most needful and natural that it should be asked: How is it, if God really meant his children thus to bring his love to their fellow-men in the way Christ brought it, by living and dying for it, how is it that the church has failed so terribly? Does God's Word actually teach and claim such entire devotion? Is it indeed an attainable degree of grace, a state that can actually be realised? Or must we not take into account the weakness of human nature, and consider the present state of the church as about all that could really be expected? We must indeed take into account the weakness of human nature. But only in a much greater degree than is usually done. It must be seen that human weakness is such utter impotence that it makes the life of God on earth an utter impossibility except as the super-natural power of the working of God's Spirit is waited on and experienced. And if the question be again asked how it is, if the declarations of God's Word are so plain, that this power of God's Spirit is not more sought and known, the answer leads us again to what we have called the root evil of the low state of the church. It is because God's wonderful commands and promises are all under-stood and accepted in a certain human sense, and not in their divine quickening meaning and power.

Let us turn to our text again, and see what a difference it would make if God's Spirit really revealed to us its divine meaning. Look at the three great mysteries the words speak of – a perishing world, a loving God, a life-giving Christ.

Just pause and think of a Christian, of yourself, asking God earnestly, perseveringly, believingly, to open his eyes, and give him a vision of the perishing world, and then setting one's self in the light of God and eternity to seek a due impression of its state. You might begin with numbers. It is known that at least 100,000 souls pass out of the darkness of heathenism into the darker eternity every day. That means more than one every second. While we are enjoying ourselves, there they drop, moment by moment, over the precipice, in utter ignorance of God and his love. And there are of such in the world a thousand million, all living and dying in this darkness. Our text says 'that whosoever believeth might not perish'! Without Christ they must perish. Think of all the inconceivable sin and wretchedness the life on earth implies and then of all the hopelessness for the world to come. Read some missionary book, giving an account of some special mission field, with definite statements as to the need, and say to God you really want to know the world in which you are placed, of which you are part, for which you are to live. Unless we study the world and take its condition in, we cannot possibly know God's love for it, or our calling.

Or think of what Scripture says of the god of this world, of the terrible power that absolutely possesses and rules these souls, and holds them in darkness and misery, and find out wherein the power and awfulness of heathenism consists. Or look nearer home, to the ungodly masses in every Christian country. Take time to consider the state of the unconverted you know, the friends you love, the people you deal with, the thousand faces that are familiar, and regard them all as making up the perishing world, in the midst of which you are to be a shining light, a streaming fountain of life. Then you will begin to see that it needs time, and trouble, and heart, and prayer to take in the divine meaning of this word 'world', and that other word 'whosoever' which is its only hope.

Then think of the loving God. This world he made for himself, to be his joy and his glory. Its sin is to him such a grief that he almost repented having made it. The suffering and the wretchedness of his creatures are to him such a sorrow that there is nothing he can do, consistent with leaving to them the freewill and the power of self-determination with which he had endowed them as part of his own image, which he would not do. He proved it by giving his own son. In a love which passeth knowledge, a love of which our conception is so utterly inadequate – that we feel so satisfied with them – his heart flows out in unceasing compassion an yearning to save and bless. On every one of these perishing millions the love of God is resting. The mind cannot take it in, but the Holy Spirit could enable the heart to know if we would only give ourselves to wait on God for this love to fill us.

The love of God has proved itself in the gift of the Son, of himself. In sending Christ to become man God proved that he longed to have man one with himself, that all his life and love as God was for man, that man might be made partaker of the divine nature. And the wonderful, the blessed 'whosoever' of our text says that that love is for every creature. The lowest, the most degraded and rejected and utterly hopeless – the love is for him, the love longs for him and is able to triumph over him. Jesus Christ came into the world for the one sole purpose of revealing this love. He spoke of it, he lived for it, he died to bring it to us. It was his one aim, his one glory, the passion and strength of his life. It was his very life; it possessed him, and he knew no other joy. And as he prayed 'that the love wherewith thou hast loved me may be in them', he meant his disciples just as much as himself, to have it in them, to live for it, to find their glory and blessedness in carrying it and making it known.

And now think of this life-giving Christ. God gave him that whosoever believeth in him might not perish, but have everlasting life. The 'whosoever' and 'believe' are inseparably connected. 'But how shall they believe on him of whom they have not heard?' Did Christ fail here, and after revealing the love and winning the life make no provision for the message being made known? Verily, no. He made provision. He arranged that every believer, every member of his body, should share with him the glory and the blessedness of communicating the divine life and love. The self-propagating power, which is the mark of all life and all love, was to find its highest manifestation in his church. The life of each believer was to be a seed bringing forth fruit after its kind.

Alas, how little the church understands or teaches this – that every believer, just like every branch on a tree, exists only to bring fruit and blessing for the glory of the husbandman and the life of men. Christ gave God's love in charge to his people, entrusted himself and the eternal life to them, that everyone whom the great 'whosoever' includes might hear and live. And Christians profess to believe that the hundreds of millions are committed to their care, and must, as the most urgent and important work in the world, have the Gospel preached to them, and yet rest content in giving, out of their abundance, a few pounds a year. And their mind and heart and strength they give to the interests of time. They have no conception of the true Christian life, of the calling and the glory and the blessedness of, like Christ, living as the channels of God's love to a perishing world.

We do indeed need a great, a mighty revival. Let us plead with God that it may begin with ourselves in secret. It will reveal to us the force of the three great words – the perishing world, God's saving love, and the Christ who through his members carries life to that world. However ignorant we may be of what we ought to do, or impotent to do what we see of this great work, let us offer ourselves unceasingly to God, to live for nothing less than what he lives for, he will inspire and guide and make us bold. When the great revival begins in our own hearts, it has begun and it will spread. We shall have new confidence in prayer and new power in work. And our work will have a new joy as we realise how it is the devotion to a great cause, which has its beginning in the love of God, its law in the life of Christ, its strength in the power of that Holy Spirit who makes us one with him in the work of conquering the world for God.

Chapter 9

God

'*For of him, and through him, and to him, are all things: to whom be glory for ever. Amen.*'
Romans 11:36

The revival is to come from God; all that it is to work is to be wrought through him; its aim and end is to lead up to him, to give us more of him, his presence and power, in the church. The desire to know and honour, to serve and glorify God more, must be one of the moving springs of true prayer for revival. If we would know what to ask and expect in a revival, that we may be prepared for what it is to bring, let our very first study be, what the place is God ought to have in his church and the believer. As we learn from what it means that to each of us and at all times, God, with his will and his kingdom, is to be all in all, we shall begin to see how greatly a revival is needed and what it is we must desire to bring – nothing less than the restoration of God to his place in his church. When God takes the place in the heart and life of each believer that he ought to have, or, let us say even less, when each believer with his whole heart longs that God should have that place, the revival will have brought its blessing to the church, and have prepared it for being a blessing to the world as it never yet has been. And why should we be content with anything less?

'Of him, and through him, and to him, are all things.' This is the God of whom we say: 'To whom be glory for ever.' This is his glory, and it is giving him glory when we know, and acknowledge, and live, and act on this blessed truth. All things are of him, as their beginning and alone author; and through him, as their continuance and maintenance, the only power by which they exist and act; and to him, as the sole aim and end for which they are have their being. This is God's glory: to know this and to make it known, to show it forth and find our blessedness in it – this is living to the glory of God. It was for this life man was created. It was to bring him back to this again that he was redeemed. This will be the highest glory of the final consummation of all things, when the Son shall have delivered up the kingdom to God, even the Father, and shall himself be subject, unto him that put all things under him, and God shall be all in all. It was for this the Son lived and died and rose again. It is for this for which he gave his people his Holy Spirit. The only true and full Christian life is that which makes this its aim. It is to restore nothing less the revival must be sought for. Let us, as a preparation for our prayer for revival, try to take what it means – this wonderful glory of the three-in-one God. Of him, and through him, and to him, are all things. He is all. He works all. He claims all.

1. God is all. God alone hath life, because he alone hath it in himself. He is the life of all that lives. The heavens and the earth are but his garment, a vesture that he changeth as he will. He alone remaineth, the everlasting one who changeth not. He is the great 'I am that I am.' The heaven and the earth are full of his glory,

everything that exists is but the outshining of the glory of his power and goodness. Were it not that we are so worldly and blind, we should see nothing but God in the universe, all existence would be but the shadow of his presence. Instinctively and joyously we would say: God is all. God has not given to nature a life which it can have in itself, independent of him. No, it remains inseparably connected with himself, and dependent on him: in all there is God; God is all.

We should say this especially about man, made in God's image. God created him that he might, in creaturely nature and form, show forth the nature of his divine and invisible glory. God created man with the one object that in and through man he might live out his divine life in such a way that man should be the voluntary and most blessed partaker of all the divine goodness and blessedness. Every attribute of God, his righteousness and holiness, his love and compassion, his goodness and truth, his wisdom and power, were not only to rest upon man, but so to be in him that they might shine out from as his own disposition and character. They were to be his very own, accepted and appropriated and personally assimilated. And yet they were ever to be known and acknowledged as God's. He was to bear the living signature. All things of God to him and in him it was indeed to be. God is all.

The ruin of sin Christ comes to restore. Creation foretells us what redemption is to effect. Christ came to bring us to God, that God might dwell in us as he meant to dwell in Adam. The Spirit came to bring God to us, that in our very heart and life, here on this earth, God might be all in us. When Christ said of the Father and himself: 'We will come and make our abode with you'; when Paul wrote of being 'filled with all the fulness of God'; when John said, 'He that dwelleth in love dwelleth in God, and God in him'; they all referrred to a possible, to a prepared, to a promised life here on earth in which the great, holy, abiding presence of God is known in the heart. We ordinarily count it an unnatural strain, an impossible struggle, ever to maintain the sense of God's nearness. This is only because we have not yet learnt that God is all – that he created us for this very thing, that he himself might be our joy, our life, our portion. Because all things are of him, because we are of him, it can be, it should be true of us and in us – *God is all*.

2. God Works All. 'Through him are all things.' He did not only begin; he alone continues and maintains. As wonderful and mysterious as is the 'of him' is also the 'through him'. He did not, as the Deist dreams, part with a certain portion of his life and power, leaving the creature to himself and certain laws he had imposed. No, above and through all these laws he himself keeps charge as the God which worketh all in all. We want to study and realise this in its relation to the Christian life. The call to let God be all in our life, the thought of ever being able to live so that it shall be to us natural, perfect rest and happiness to walk with God and maintain unbroken communion with him, is counted a dream, an impossible ideal, an overstrained demand. And why? Simply because the 'through him all things' is not understood and believed. Men have never had their eyes opened to see that all that God has begun he himself continues; that all that he demands he himself works out; that his divine purpose as author of all carries with it the assurance that he will perfect all he began. The God whom Christ has made known is one 'who works both to will and to do', who perfects in us every good work to do his will, working in us that which is pleasing in his sight. 'Through him all things': if we really believe and seek spiritually to understand this word, what a change it would work in our spiritual life! We should begin to see how really we may follow in the footsteps of the Son of God, and expect the Father to work all for us as he did for him. He said, 'I can do nothing of myself', 'I speak not of myself, but the Father doeth the works', and taught us that the great mark of his human life was what God had meant the life of Adam to be, an unceasing dependence, an entire yielding of spirit to the Father,

waiting for and receiving his working in him. It is this disposition, 'the mind that was in Christ Jesus', the very spirit of his Son, that God sent forth into our hearts, that we might live like him.

In the life of faith there is no lessson more needful and indispensable, and yet, owing to our self-confidence, none more difficult, than that of the utter weakness and helplessness of the regenerate man to live the spiritual and truly Christlike life without the unceasing, every moment working of God's power in us through the Holy Spirit. The terrible deceit of the serpent in Paradise still lingers with us, and instead of counting the most absolute dependence on God our highest blessedness, as securing his doing all in us, we are unwilling to cease from our strength and let him work all. We either do not care, or find it hard to say, 'I will glory in my infirmities, that the power of Christ may rest upon me.' It is because the Holy Spirit has never given us the full vision of the full life. Of God, and through God all things.

Let no one think that all this lies outside the region of everyday, practical life. It is just there this truth is needed to give the victory. In a revival which is truly to lift the church to its true position, making men say, 'God is in you of a truth', nothing is so essential as that they be restored to the position for which man was created, that God be allowed to have his way with them, and to work in them all that is pleasing in his sight. As they know the God, of whom are all things, both in creation and redemption, they will honour and glorify him by the trust that through him also, in them too, are all things.

3. God Claims All. 'To him are all things.' The end ever returns to the beginning. All that comes forth from God returns to God. In the very nature of things, as all is of God and through God, all must be to him for his sake and glory. To the question, What is the chief end of man? there can be no higher answer than: To glorify God and enjoy him for ever. And how can man glorify him? Simply by making known what a glorious being he is, by proving that he is worthy to be honoured, trusted

and obeyed. And this, again, is done very specially by just yielding ourselves to God to work in us all his will. As Peter says, 'If any man minister, let him do it as of the ability which God giveth, that God in all things may be glorified through Jesus Christ.' There is no higher way of glorifying God than being his passive instrument, waiting for him to work in us, doing our work as of the ability which God giveth. The more we know that all is of God, and all through God, the more spontaneous will be the surrender of all to God. Our one aim will be to glorify God. And in glorifying God we shall enjoy him.

Many, very many Christians, may we now say most Christians, have never seen that God claims all, that he asks that every moment of our life, every power of our being, every part of our possessions, shall have but one aim – the pleasure, the glory of God. They think such a life difficult and impossible, and with that every earnest prayer or effort after it is stifled. They hold firmly to their orthodox, what they count scriptural, view of what they think possible for a Christian, and never seek for the Spirit's revelation of God's thoughts concerning the standard of a Christian life. They know very little of giving God his glory and worshipping him as the all in all; they know still less about his working all in all; no wonder that they have never understood the claim – all things to him. They, therefore, cannot say: To him be glory.

Giving God glory, glorifying God, means above all, making him and his glory known to men, so that they also give him glory. Every soul brought to know God in Christ gives him new glory. Of this it was that Jesus said: 'I have glorified thee on earth. I have finished the work thou gavest me to do. I have manifested thy name.' This work that the Father gave his Son to do, the Son has entrusted to us. As a member of Christ's body, as a Son of the living God, every believer is called to live as much for the glory of God, in the salvation of souls, as Christ was. God claims all – the whole heart and strength for his love and service. Let us study this claim. If it is true that all things are of God, there is nothing that is not from him, that is not his – everything we are and have is his – surely it is most reasonable that they should all and only be used for him. If it is true, all things through him, there is nothing that he does not uphold, empower and work, and surely he ought to have the honour and glory of it. If it is true that in his infinite love he gave his Son, his all, for us, and in him and his Spirit, himself to be our life, surely, our heart ought willingly and joyfully to say: To him, to him alone, all things, my life, too, and all I am.

This saying is hard. Is it not too much to ask that all our pleasure, all our time, all our thought, must be set on glorifying God? Alas, the question proves how little we believe that God is nothing but pure love, and goodness, and blessedness, and that no one can ever have too much of him, that the more we can have of him and his will and presence the more consummate our happiness. And yet it is just this blessedness that keeps so many from ever seriously listening to the call to come and walk with this God of whom are all things, to live wholly for him. Or else it is the other thought of unbelief, just as foolish, and dangerous, and sinful: they do not think it possible to live the life; it may be true that all things are through God, but not this; at least, not for them. They cannot think that God will work it. Their unbelief refuses to say – Yes, to him be all things, in my life, too.

Christian friend, is it not becoming clear what we need a revival for? – A new revelation of God! Not a new Bible: the revelation of God which is complete and altogether sufficient. We need a revelation about ourselves and of the church concerning the glory of God that he shall be everything to us, in very deed, all in all to us. Such a revelation of him *of whom* are all things, whose offspring we are, that in him we shall wholly live and move and have our being. Such a revelation of him *through whom* are all things, and who worketh in us by his mighty power, that our whole life will be like Christ's, one of joyful dependence and fellowship. Such a revelation of him *to whom* are all things, that it becomes impossible in the power of the Holy Spirit within us to be or wish to do anything but to him and his glory.

What a difference it would make in the world – in each place or congregation a group of Christians, consciously, spontaneously seeking to win back for God his place in the hearts of his creatures. Not our striving, alongside other interests, to do something for God and his glory, but proving, by a heart and life possessed with a passion, and sacrificing everything, for the establishment of God's kingdom among men, that to them God is all in all, that to glorify God is their chief end.

Let us believe that this is not impossible. Let us consider deeply the state of the church, as seen in the majority of Christians, and fervently pray that God will give us and them some right sense of the life he actually has a right to ask, and does expect that we should live. Let us think, and pray, and yield to the Holy Spirit's teaching until the thought that God is not known and glorified by his children as he should be becomes unbearable, and we are thrown upon him in the pleading of an urgent and assured faith that God is able, that God is waiting to reveal his glory to his people.

Chapter 10

Sin

'*Sin abounded ... sin reigned ... sin slew me
... that through the commandment sin might
become exceeding sinful.*'
Romans 5:20–21; 7:11, 13

The evil of sin, its exceeding sinfulness, consists in this
one thing, that it is committed against God. It is the
denial and rejection of God; it grieves and hurts him; it
is the death of all that is of him. The measure of our
knowledge of God will be the measure of our sense of
sin. It is our participation in the Spirit of God which will
alone fit us for knowing what sin really is.

It has been said that one of the characteristics of our
age, of its life and thought and theology, is the lack of a
sense of sin. And also that any deep spiritual revival
must be preached by a deeper sense of sin. A deeper
sense of sin means personal conviction and humiliation.
We need to ask God by his Holy Spirit to convict his

people about sin. In its influence on ourselves, one of the most terrible effects of sin is that it is blind to its own nature, and makes us incapable of knowing what it is and how evil. It is only the Spirit of God who knows the things of God, and his hatred and judgment of sin, who can give us a true sense of what sin is. The Spirit can give us in some measure to know what God's sense of sin is.

To reveal this was one of the great objects of Christ's coming into the world. 'If I had not come, they had not had sin, but now they have no excuse for their sin.' In Christ's sense of sin we learn what ours ought to be. In him as man the sense of sin is seen in his determination not to do it; in his refusal and condemnation of it; in his readiness to die to have it conquered and cast out. He had such a sense of sin that he gave his life to conquer it. The deep sense of sin will be seen in us too in the readiness rather to die than do it, rather to die than that others should do it. Yes, more actually to die with him to sin and all that is under its power, to the world and the flesh, is the only way to the full experience of the divine liberty from its power in ourselves and others. It is when something of this sense of sin in our holy Lord comes to us, that that element of which he could not have, will come to us in all its power – the anguish of having sinner and having a nature that is entirely sinful. It is in the hatred of actual sinning, in the battle against it as well as in the knowledge and abhorrence of the incurable evil of our earthly nature and the victory over it, that the true sense of sin will be fostered and proved. As we now consider what the Word teaches about sin and how God would have us to think about it, and behave towards it, let us yield to the Holy Spirit, the Spirit of judgment and the Spirit of burning, to make sin exceedingly sinful to us, and to show us what to think about the church in this connection.

Consider its entrance into the world. Out of the chaos which there is every reason to believe was caused by the fall of the angels, God created a new world, which man was to rule and to keep from the power of those who had lost it. When the old serpent succeeded in tempting our first parents to disobey, to throw off their allegiance to God, and listen to him, he became their master. In conquering them he regained his power over the world that had been entrusted to them, and became the god of this world.

The origin of sin, as having come through the temptation of Satan, teaches us two things of infinite importance. It makes deliverance possible. If man had sinned of himself from within he would have been a devil without hope. It shows us the dark background of all sin. Let us not look at single acts of sin, or at the sinful nature, but at the living mighty power that is behind it all, instigating it, giving it its hideousness and heinousness as actual enmity and resistance to God, binding and holding men as its slaves.

Consider its nature. God had created man for nothing less than to be his habitation, in whom he might dwell and rest and delight, through whom he might show forth his goodness and glory by making man a sharer in both. What God intended was that his divine life should live within the human life, inspiring all its actions. In a voluntary and most blessed dependence man was to unceasingly offer his selfhood, his power of self-determination, to God, to have his will, his affections, his mind, all filled with God. Satan's temptation was that man should seek his own pleasure and do his own will, should turn from God to self as his leader. When man listened self took the place of God, and since that day self has been the fountain of every sin that has ever been committed. 'Is it to be self or God?' is still day by day the question to which sin gives its terible answer, while men but little think that their sin means. What is said of the man of sin, the fruit and outcome of the development of sin, its incarnation, 'Who opposeth and exalteth himself above all that is called God,' is true, in principle, of every sin. Self exalting itself above God! May God open our eyes and hearts to see and believe it.

Consider its evil. The evil of sin is that it is committed

against God. God is our Creator; he made us; we belong to him. God made us for himself, in his own image and likeness, capable of fellowship with himself and the full participation in all his glory. God is love; he had no thought but of filling us with his own divine blessedness. It is this God sin rejects. Instead of loving, worshipping, pleasing him, we grieve, we hurt, we provoke him. Yes, this is the evil of sin; we have compelled God to rise up in the fierceness and anger of his holy wrath against sin and evil, and let them come upon us, the creature he made and loved.

If we would know the evil of sin let us look to heaven. From all eternity God could never do anything but hate sin as an accursed thing. And now that we join ourselves to that accursed thing and live in it, that curse rests on us. God's sentence of death is on us. God's justice is our enemy.

Consider the effect of sin in man. It ruined man's whole nature. His body at once became the prey of corrupt and disordered passions. His darkened mind thought to hide himself from God behind the trees, to cover his shame with fig leaves, to excuse himself by casting blame on others. His spirit had lost its peace with God and its power of fellowship with him. Life, the life of God, with all the infinite meaning of that word, had been his destiny; and now death, spiritual, temporal, eternal, is his portion. The sentence and the power of death is on him; to God and to goodness he is dead. Think of the individual, in his impotence to do good, in his estrangement from his God, in all the wretchedness and misery he can suffer. Think of the ruin and wretchedness sin has brought into the world during all these long ages. Think of the dark, dark eternity, where the power of sin is to have its full manifestation. And ask whether the church sufficiently believes and teaches how unspeakably awful sin is.

Consider the power of sin. I am not thinking so much of the race and its universal dominion, but of the extent to which it has obtained possession of and mastered the

whole being of man. Its supremacy is absolute. Men
deny this, and point to so much that is good and noble
and beautiful in many a man who knows not, or knowing, rejects God. Most true; the remnants, the broken
fragments, the ruins of the temple God had made for
himself are still beautiful, the proofs of its original glory.
But still it is a temple no longer; the wild beasts and
creeping things lodge there. That which alone consti-
tuted man's spiritual worth, loving God with all his
heart, being a home in which God could dwell and work,
that is lost. Sin has taken the place of God; in the midst
of, yes, for this is the sad truth, even over that which is
still beautiful, sin reigns. Even the most sacred of our
natural affections and the most beautiful of our virtues
are stained and spoiled by sin. Nowhere is this seen more
clearly than just in the Christian who has been regener-
ated by God's own Holy Spirit. As the new nature grows
in the knowledge of God's will and in the desire to do it,
the discovery is gradually made of how self does indeed
pervade all, and how, through self, sin has spread its
power through our whole being. And the Christian
learns that as truly as God was cast out and sin took his
place, sin can only be cast out by God in Christ taking its
place, and each moment, by a personal indwelling, and
an unceasing operation, maintaining the new nature in
power. And so deliverance from sinning in sanctification
only comes as the Holy Spirit each moment reveals and
imparts the saving power of the indwelling Christ. As
complete as in creation the divine and indwelling was
meant to be, the indwelling of sin became. As complete
as that became, the sanctifying indwelling and presence
of God must be, if the power of sin is to be kept from
asserting dominion.

Consider the deliverance from sin. Nothing will reveal
its terrible nature and power more than this. So entire
has been the corruption and the ruin of man's nature that
there is no cure for it but death – the entire bringing to an
end, the destruction, of the old life, the impartation of
an entirely new life, come down from God in heaven. It

was for this that Christ had to die. 'Our old man was crucified with him.' He had to bear its punishment and its condemnation; he had in death to submit to its curse as God's righteous judgment on sin, and so by his atonement to destroy its power. He had to show that there was no way out from under the power of sin and death and the curse, but by dying to it; giving up the life over which it had had power, and receiving a new life from God. So he opened for us a new and living way to God – that we, being dead with him, dead to sin and the world, to self and all that is our our sinful nature, might live unto God. Yes, so deep is the corruption of our nature, so entirely is every part of it, however beautiful and true and good it appears to men, under the power of sin, that nothing but the daily death to what is of self and nature, the daily abiding in Christ's death, and carrying about the death of the Lord Jesus in our mortal bodies, can give the full experience of his power to save ourselves and others. As the standard by which to judge sin is the death of Christ, so the standard by which to judge our sense of sin is our willingness to die to it. Like Christ, rather die than sin; with Christ indeed die that we may be freed from it – let this be the test of our thought and our hatred of sin.

And what is now the bearing of all this on the coming revival among Christians, and our prayer for it? I have already quoted the saying: Any deep spiritual revival must needs be preceded and accompanied by a deeper sense of sin. That does not only mean a deeper intellectual apprehension in our theology of what sin is. Nor a deeper expression of self-abhorrence on account of the sin that is still in our nature. It will include these two things. But it will mean much more. It will specially mean a deeper sense of the ordinary sins we still commit. It will mean that the Holy Spirit will, as he once convicted us of sin for conversion, convict us of sin for sanctification, showing us the mind of God concerning sins of temper, of the flesh, of pride and selfishness, or worldliness and half-heartedness and disobedience. Just as the conviction of sin, whether individual sins, or of our sins as a whole, led up to the insight that they were not, as we had thought, the mere result of weaknesss, but as sin of unbelief, the rejection of Christ in not accepting his deliverance, so this will be still more the case when the Holy Spirit convicts God's children of sin in preparation for revival. Things that have been tolerated, as if they were a necessity owing to our weakness, things that we have become so accustomed to that we hardly notice them, will be revealed as sin because they prove that we have not allowed him to work in us what he would. As the ignorance of the Jews of him whom they had crucified was not counted as an excuse for their sin, our ignorance and weakness will not avail in the burning searching of the Holy Spirit. Sin will be seen and felt to be a proof that Christ is not fully accepted as prince and saviour, that the surrender to his will and the trust in his grace has not been whole-hearted. It is the measure of our surrender to Christ to be freed from sinning that is the measure of our sense of sin. The determination at all costs to be kept from sinning is the proof of our hatred of it. The deepening sense of sin will manifest itself in the intensity of our clinging to him who delivers from it.

'Ye know that he was manifested to take away sin.' That does not only refer to atonement, but specially to actual sinning, for John adds at once, 'He that abideth in him sinneth not.' The truest sense of sin will come to him who seeks and has the fullest deliverance from it. As long as there is any quarter given to the secret thought of a necessity of sinning, the true sense of sin cannot prevail. When it is seen that the faith in a remainder of sin in the flesh and faith in the continual triumph over sin are not irreconcilable, and that Christ can keep the believer evermore living a life in his keeping, without any commission of known or wilful sin, or any wilful desire for what is wrong, the sin and the shame of still committing sin against such a Lord will become intolerable.

What a revelation from God it will need to show his people the sinfulness of sin: 'the abominable thing which my soul hateth'. And what a revelation to show them the sins which are so heedlessly tolerated in the church! And what a revelation to show how he is able in mighty power to deal with sin and deliver from it! And what a revelation to show how the whole of nature, with all that we regard as indifferent and neutral, has the stain and stamp of sin upon it, and needs the power of Christ and his Holy Spirit filling the life to make it holy! And what a revelation to make us see that the measure of his mighty sanctifying grace is the measure of the sinfulness of the sin we now commit!

If the Holy Spirit is to work in power for the revival of believers, some, at least, must be convicted of the sins that are withholding the blessing. Let us offer ourselves to God to bear the burden of the sins of his people. Let us cry to God to show us and them what his judgment is of the state of his church. Let us confess by name, in deep humility and love, the sins we see. Let us pray fervently for a deep sense of the sin of the world, of the church, of our own life, that our prayer for revival may become an urgent, intense, believing, prevailing cry for God to discover sin and so be delivered from it.

Chapter 11

Deliverance from Sin

> '*Ye know that he was manifested to take away sins; and in him is no sin. Whosoever abideth in him sinneth not … Whosoever is begotten of God doeth no sin, because his seed abideth in him: and he cannot sin, because he is begotten of God.*' 1 John 3:5–9

The name 'Keswick teaching' is now universally used to denote a certain well-defined line of teaching. The novelty and peculiarity of that teaching consists not in any new truth it has to offer, but in the prominence it gives to truths that have been allowed to lie dormant. From this many have been led to say that, if Keswick has no truth that is not the common heritage of all evangelical churches, it cannot have any secret of power or blessing that is not to be found elsewhere. Men forget that it is not the doctrine that a church has in its creeds, or a minister in his teaching. That is the measure of power, but only so much of it as is being made living truth in the experience of teacher and hearer and the power of the Holy Spirit. Keswick teaching owes the wonderful influence it has exercised to the fact that its founder called believers together to come and hear him, and others who had been blessed with him, to tell them what God had done for their souls. And all along the keynote of its platform has been personal testimony to what God has done and is doing in giving power over sin. It is only as this secret of its power is apprehended that its wonderful influence can be understood or appreciated. No one has a right to demand that all Christians shall state their views in the same way as the Keswick speakers do. Much less would say one claim that without this the same blessing cannot be expected from above. But there are certain great principles which lie at the very root of the testimony and the teaching that has been so fruitful, and which do appear to be esssential to all growth in holiness, to which all teachers and believers who are longing and labouring for the revival of the church would do well to give, in all their prayer and faith, the same definite prominence which has made them such a blessing.

1. The first of these truths is that concerning sin. It is founded on texts such as the one we have chosen. Christ was manifested to take away sin – not only guilt, but sin. To this end he is the sinless one, that a soul abiding in him does not sin; a man born of God 'doth not and cannot sin, for his seed abideth in him.' The seed is the life power out of which a tree grows, and which abides in it. In the power of the divine life the born of God cannot commit sin. All three expressions, 'sinneth not, doth not sin, cannot sin,' refer to deeds, to actual transgressions. They say nothing about the flesh, the sinful nature still present in the believer. That is not the question dealt with here; they appear simply to hold out the promise that from the committal of actual sin the believer who abides in Christ can be kept.

If anyone would really understand Keswick teaching he must get hold of this thought: that the desire to be kept from sinning, and the prospect held out of being taught how to come to this, is its great attraction. I have seen appreciative notices of Keswick Conventions, one hears and reads beautiful articles and addresses on the fuller and the deeper life, in which this, the very root-thought of all true holiness teaching, appears to be left out. One has only to go back to the life of Canon Battersby, the founder of Keswick, to see the truth of what I say. He had for more than twenty years been a minister of deeply evangelical views, and of a beautiful Christian character. And yet he was dissatisfied. Sins of tongue and of temper, of worldliness and self-will, came from time to time to cloud communion with God, and to rob him of his peace. When first he heard in 1873 of the teaching of a higher life, with the promise of being kept continually by Christ in victory over sin, he longed greatly to know if this were really possible. At the same time he feared much the thought of sinless perfection, and dreaded being led into anything that would not be consistent with scriptural truth as to a holiness never to be found in ourselves, but in Christ alone. This state of his mind is evident from what he writes in his journal, September 1873: 'What I have been reading of the experience of others has made me utterly dissatisfied with myself and my state. I feel that I am dishonouring God and am wretched by living as I do, and that I must either go backward or forward, reaching out towards the light which my Saviour holds out to me, or falling back more and more into worldliness and sin.'

It was this weariness with a life of continual struggling and failure, of continual humbling and sinning, that prepared Canon Battersby for the teaching he heard given at the Oxford Convention, 1874, and made the invitation to come to Jesus and rest in him for keeping from sin and the power of holiness like a new gospel. What was taught as to what Christ would do in keeping and saving continually, as to the faith that dared trust him for thus keeping and saving, as much as for pardon, gave him boldness to claim and accept all that Christ could do.

And as, in the midnight hour, after a meeting, he gave himself to the Lord, he had such a revelation of what Jesus is and will be to a trusting soul, that ever after he could only speak of it with tender reverence. But the teaching and the revelation owed its power and its preciousness entirely to this one thing: it was a felt need – an intense longing not to sin, to be freed from the daily so-called little sins that cloud our communion with God. It is this fact that explains why at Keswick such prominence is given to the exposure of the infirmities and failings of Christians. As the Holy Spirit is allowed to convict of sin in regard to such things, the sense of impotence and bondage is awakened, and the desire stirred for a life of liberty and power. If we are to have a great work of the Holy Spirit in power among believers, it will have to begin here. The sins that they have borne with all too contentedly, because they thought that no deliverance is possible, must be revealed by God's Word and the Holy Spirit as a shame and a guilt, a grief and dishonour to Christ, the cause of failure in our own prayers and our labours. It is only when this is felt aright that the Holy Spirit can manifest Christ in all his saving power.

2. As the first truth we have spoken of is the longing for deliverance from the committal of actual sin, so the second is, that Scripture promises, and that grace has made abundant provision for, a life in which there is power to cease from the doing of sin. The whole church unites in the confession: Christ saves from the guilt and power of sin, but the preaching and the testimony of experience has been far clearer in regard to the former than the latter. At the Reformation it was most natural that all attention should be fixed on the one great truth of justification by faith. But a great mistake was made when in succeeding generations this truth was treated as if it were the whole gospel. As a consequence a great deal of evangelical teaching has been defective and one-sided, and a great deal of evangelical living has been marked by anything but a high standard of righteousness and holiness. 'In him is no sin ... he that abideth in him

sinneth not' – the words that were given to shed light and hope on our path are counted a riddle. Canon Battersby lived for eight years after he found the blessed secret he had so long sought. His testimonies at Keswick and his private journals prove that he knew that he had not been deceived in the experience he passed through. He never thought for a moment that the sinful nature had been eradicated. He never professed that he had been perfectly free from sinful acts. But what he did know and confess was that his entire life in its relation to sin had been changed – that he had entered upon a walk in the light and liberty of Christ he had never known before, and that when for a moment, owing to a lack of perfect trust, there was a fall, there was the presence of Christ for immediate restoration to the life of peace and power. The whole tenor of his life was in the freedom from known sin in a degree entirely unknown in his previous experience. This is nothing else but what George Müller means when he so frequently speaks of being enabled by the grace of God to have a good conscience, not knowingly doing anything against the will of God. I cannot insist too strongly that the reason that so many seek in vain so earnestly for the mighty strengthening of the Spirit in the inner man, and the promised manifestation of Christ which comes through the Spirit, is owing to this, that they do not seek Christ for which he is first and last – a saviour from sin. It is the deep longing, the humble expectation, the determined purpose, to be saved from the common daily sins, that is the only true preparation for the revelation of the Lord Jesus in the soul.

3. In connection with this there comes another truth so much emphasised at Keswick – the need of a new and entire surrender to Christ. Christ's work as our sanctification and his keeping us from sin, rests on the fact of his being our life, and his having entire possession and control of our being. It depends on our being entirely given up to him and following him with such wholeheartednesss that we leave him free to do with us and to work in us what he pleases. A defective insight into the impor-

tance of this is the cause of much unavailing prayer and effort. Souls long to be delivered from some particular form of sin. They come and confess and surrender it, or that portion of their nature in which it roots. And yet they forget that it avails little to take away an ugly branch of a tree, if root and stem still remain. It is no good, it is often great harm, to deal with the symptoms of a disease itself. When Christ asks that the offending member shall be cut off, this is only as a part of the large requirement, to forsake all and follow him. His demand of those who would know his power to save and keep from sinning is that, in a sense, and to an extent they never thought needful or possible, they shall live with him, and for him, and in him – their whole life actually under his management and inspiration, wholly dependent on and subjected to him.

It is nothing less than this is meant by abiding in him. 'In him is no sin. He that abideth in him sinneth not.' The abiding in him, the sinless one, in which is implied the going out of all of self and its life, to wait and dwell in his will and strength, brings the power that does not commit sin. Through the revelation and fellowship of the Holy Spirit the presence of Christ becomes a divine reality. He dwells in the heart to root it in love and fill it with the fullness of God. The one condition is – a life entirely surrendered to Christ – a heart wholly occupied with him, seeking nothing for itself except as a means of honouring and serving him.

Of this surrender one thing more must be said. Though it must be a disposition, a lifelong habit and state of the heart, maintained by the grace of the Holy Spirit, the entrance upon it may be very often the work of a moment. As with so many who came to Christ with their petitions on earth, when the need becomes urgent, and the power and will of Christ are understood, and the sinner is ready at Christ's word to obey and accept, the conscious deliverance may be immediate. One step is enough to turn from the path where we have stumbled along in our own strength, to the highway of holiness where Jesus keeps the feet of his saints.

4. The last truth of Keswick teaching that must not be omitted is that of the power of faith. The whole evangelical church is one in the confession that salvation is by faith alone. But that every part of that salvation, sanctification equally with justification by faith, has been too much overlooked. All that has been said above of liberty from sinning, of the entire surrender to Christ and abiding in him, of his indwelling and keeping, and the continuous life of his Holy Spirit, with all the power these truths have exercised in thousands of lives, is dependent upon the one great truth – all things are possible to him that believeth. When the first call comes to the believer to make a new and entire surrender as the condition of knowing the saving power of Jesus fully, he generally feels how formidable it is to make such a surrender with any hope of its being true or lasting. He stands baffled at the thought of an impossible demand, until he sees that for the ability to make the surrender Christ can be trusted. When he is taught that the new life he is to enter on is to be one of faith that moment by moment rests in the Lord, he again is all fear, but he should not have such continual faith until he sees how he can trust Christ to keep his very faith from failing. When the thought comes of daily temptation to sin, he has to learn that each difficulty will vanish in the presence of faith, because faith is the committal of our need to a faithful Saviour. And so with every promise of the Spirit's fullness, or the Saviour's indwelling, or the life of fruitfulness and blessing, he learns that because God is to work all, faith is the one disposition which secures every blessing. Saved by faith – becomes moment by moment the watchword of his life.

But how is it that men who bear the name of believers find it so hard, and so often fail, to be believers indeed? Why were those who came to Christ on earth so soon brought to believe in his word of healing, and why do we, with our greater light, the power of the Holy Spirit, the beginnings of faith in our heart, lose so much by our unbelief? The answer is simple, but very significant. Those men felt their need, and longed with their whole heart to be freed from their disease. The disease was the one burden of their life; deliverance from it their one desire. They were ready to believe. When daily sinning becomes the burden of our life, and deliverance from it our one desire, the message, 'he that abideth in him sinneth not', will get a new attraction. And the testimony of those who can say that they once knew what is was to carry that burden, but that they have found a deliverance beyond what they dared hope for, will waken a longing that will leave no rest. As we pray for revival, let us pray much for a conviction of sin, through the Spirit, in believers that will make the daily sins unbearable. That will prepare for a revelation of Christ, through the Spirit, that will call out a surrender and a faith to which he can give himself and his life in full measure.

Chapter 12

The Sickly and the Healthy Life

'We are the circumcision, who worship by the Spirit of God, and glory in Christ Jesus, and have no confidence in the flesh.'
Philippians 3:3

In more than one chapter I have spoken of the two levels of Christian walk, and the necessity of our living on the higher, which is simply the true Christian life, if we are to get the victory over our failures, and enter upon the path we can become faithful and strong in prayer. The question is often asked whether and where these two stages are to be found in Scripture. I feel an insight into this to be of such importance that I will try and give as simple and clear an answer as possible.

That answer is you find it everywhere. The difference is simply that which we see around us between a healthy and a sickly man. Both are living men, with all the attributes that go to make up a man. But the one is able to fulfil his duty as a man, and to do so joyfully and successfully. To the other the performance of duty is a burden, if not an impossibility, because he is out of health and lacks the needful strength. And even so when Scripture divides Christians into carnal and spiritual, those who remain babes when they ought to be men, and those who have gone on unto perfection or maturity, into those who walk after the flesh and those who walk after the Spirit, those who live under the law and its bondage and those who live as under grace, and the liberty and joy it gives, it points to the two possible states of a believer living either a feeble, sickly life, or a life of health and vigour. Once we see this, every command to live up to the privileges of our state, every promise about the full salvation which the Holy Spirit can work, every warning about yielding to self and the flesh, becomes a call to us to decide which of the two styles of living shall be ours.

All the teaching in the epistles is founded on the solemn thought of a Christian having the opportunity and the power to decide whether he will live after the flesh or after the Spirit, whether he will live a half-hearted, half-worldly life, or yield himself wholly to be led by the Spirit. In the Epistle to the Galatians, for instance, Paul does not only call Christians to abstain from sin, both in its grosser form, or in what are considered its lesser and more pardonable, almost inevitable manifestations, as anger, or envy, or strife, but he seeks to bring home to them that their sins are the works of an evil power, the flesh, and are the proof that they are under its rule. He does not only teach them to seek love and joy and gentleness and temperance, but points out that these are the fruit of the Spirit, and how everything therefore depends upon their knowing under which law they are living, that of the flesh or of the Spirit. A man may be striving most earnestly to conquer certain sins, but until the axe is laid to the root of the tree, and he sees that he must be brought out from under the power of the flesh unto the liberty of the Spirit, his efforts will be comparatively vain.

Let us in this light consider the teaching of Scripture. Take a command like that of our Lord: 'Abide in me, and I in you.' Does not the very need of such an injunction prove that a man may be in Christ, and yet, through ignorance or sloth or unbelief, fail of that purposeful conscious abiding which brings forth much fruit and has power in prayer. Christ's command at once draws a dividing line. Those who in faith surrender their whole being to let him work in them all he will, occupy an entirely different platform from those who are not ready then to forsake all and follow fully. These latter do not fail of salvation, but only the former have the spiritual capacity to prove fully the power of the prayer promises.

Or take the teaching of Paul in Romans 6: 'How shall we who died to sin, any longer live therein? Reckon yourselves to be indeed dead unto sin, and alive unto God in Christ Jesus. Yield yourselves unto God, as alive from the dead.' Does not the teaching at once suggest the thought that there might be Christians at Róme who were ignorant of these truths, and as a consequence, could not be living in the experience of their power? Is it not the case that very many Christians regard this epistle up to the fifth chapter, with its blessed truths of justification, as the very key of the Gospel while they look upon chapter 6 as beyond their reach both in thought and experience? And does it not follow that a believer who has by the Holy Spirit's power yielded himself as dead to sin and alive in God must have a secret power of victory over sin which the other cannot have?

The words that follow, in verses 14 and 15, only bring this out more clearly. 'Shall we sin ... ?' This is the great question of the chapter. 'Shall we sin, because we are not under the law but under grace?' The very question shows that a believer may misunderstand the meaning of what grace is and does. He may think of grace chiefly as pardon; he may not know that grace is able and ready to work in him all he needs for obedience or holiness; such a defective view must hinder his spiritual life. Because he does not know and prove the fullness of grace, he naturally acts under the law and its bondage. It cannot be otherwise: there are only these two powers, law and grace; whatever in my being is not under the actual and active reign of grace working in me under the power of law with its ceaseless appeal to self-effort. It is not evident that here there must be two entirely distinct modes of Christian living, and that until the believer is brought out entirely from under the law and led to see that there is a life in which grace really every moment works everything, he cannot live the healthy vigorous life of the man who practically knows the glorious liberty of the sons of God.

Just one more illustration. Take from Romans 8 or Galatians 5 an expression like 'led by the Spirit', 'walk in the Spirit.' Many Christians will confess that they have but a very vague idea of what the work of the Holy Spirit in them is. They do not know that he is the Spirit of grace, the Spirit through whose presence and energy in them, moment by moment, the work of grace can be maintained for every possible need of their spiritual life. They do not know that they may realize his presence continually by faith, and so live a life in everything yielded up to himself personally for guidance and strength. It is not plain that a believer to whom all this has been brought home as a matter of living faith and experience must be living on an entirely different level from him who is struggling in his own strength, all the while he asks God to help him?

Listen to words like these: 'Walk by the Spirit, and ye shall not fulfil the lusts of the flesh. If ye are led by the Spirit, ye are not under law. If ye through the Spirit do mortify the deeds of the body, ye shall live.' Do they not all indicate clearly that there is a spiritual life in which many of the Galatians were not living, and to which Paul was calling them? To be under the law, to walk after the flesh, that is, in our own strength, even in religious things, so as to make a fair show in the flesh, is a state of sickliness and failure; to have crucified the flesh, to walk by the Spirit, and to be filled with the fruit of the Spirit is the true life to which we are called, truly possible and most blessed.

My Christian friend, I cannot but think that if you will carefully consider such passages, and I might cite many others, you will see what abundant reason there is for speaking of the two stages in the Christian life. And then you will see of what importance it is to insist upon it, and upon your confessing in which of these two you are. As long as people refuse to do this to themselves, their hurt will not be healed. They will ever be trying to deal with individual sins, and not know that their failure in doing so is because there is something radically wrong. They are still struggling in their own strength; they have not yet entered upon the life of simple and entire trust in Christ to work all in them by his Holy Spirit. Even if they admit that there is much defective in these respects, they will strive to be more faithful, they will watch against that accursed self that leads them away, they will seek to trust and pray more earnestly for promised grace. They hope to grow out of it into something better. They forget that we can grow out of feebleness into strength, but that for sick men we need the medicine or the knife of the physician. It is only as we fully accept the teaching of God's Word in regard to the two possible ways of living that are open to the Christian that we shall really see that an entire transition from the one to the other is a possibility, and why it is that that transition can be the work of a single moment.

Here is another great difficulty with many. They cannot understand how a single step can effect such a change. May the Lord help me to make it plain.

Just listen. Suppose some one at Rome, reading one of the texts we have quoted, 'Ye are not under the law, but under grace', had his eyes all at once opened to see that he had never fully known what grace was, but had been living in bondage under the law, what ought he to have done? Suppose he had met Paul later, and had asked him what he ought to do. Would not the answer have been: At once, this very moment, yield to grace, and trust it to do its work in you? Paul writes: 'Therefore it is of grace, that it may be by faith.' And whatever is to be believed, because it is true, is to be believed at once. The message has come to you, to see whether the oft-repeated failure in your prayer life, and the feeling of hopelessness with regard to any very great change in it being possible, be not owing to your having sought under the law to fulfil God's demands in your own strength, and not having known the joy of the Holy Spirit as your strength. I pray you, beware of now resolving not to look to your own strength any more, to pray more and to trust more. It will be healing your hurt slightly, dealing with certain symptoms of disease, without touching the root of the evil. Be not ashamed of confessing that your life, as a whole, has been on the wrong level, that it needs entire reconstruction, and that it is only the almighty power of Christ that can bring you into the faith where all your walk will be by faith alone. The deeper your sense, and the fuller your admission, of the wrongness of your present state, notwithstanding all God has done for you and in you, the clearer will be your conviction that nothing but work of God can put you right, and the bolder your faith to claim it from him at once.

To take another illustration from the Galatians. Suppose one of them had asked Paul: I confess that, though I have believed in Christ, I have been walking after the flesh, and living under the law. How am I to come from under it, and live as one who walks in the Spirit, and is led by the Spirit? Would the answer not be clear and decisive – Have I not written you (3:14) 'We receive the promise of the Spirit by faith.' Will you not at once confess and forsake the folly of having sought anything in yourself or the law, and believe that this life in the leading of the Holy Spirit is yours? It is no other answer we need. When once we yield to the Holy Spirit's conviction of sin, of the sin of unbelief, in not having trusted Christ, his grace and his Spirit, to do all in us, as the only possible cause of failure, every difficulty will disappear, and we shall joyfully accept the message that our only hope is in the immediate surrender to Christ to do all the work in us, because we now see that he will do it all.

Let us now turn to our text and consider the contrast, the warning, the example, the promise. The contrast points to those who were not the true circumcision, Christians who did not know what it was to have no confidence in the flesh. The warning comes to us, to fear and beware lest our Christian life, with all its zeal and all we have known of grace, may be suffering from the same disease. Let us not think of the Judaising party in the early church. Legality is the religion of human nature, the very last thing the flesh will give up, and from which nothing but the full life of the Spirit can free us. The example is bright and clear: Paul says of himself and his friends, those like-minded with himself, whom he later calls the perfect (Phil 3:15), the mature, 'We are the circumcision', our hearts circumcised by the Lord our God in the putting off of the body of the flesh, 'who worship by the Spirit of God and glory in Christ Jesus, and have no confidence in the flesh.' There is a life possible – we see it here – in which we are made free from all secret trust in the flesh; in which we wholly live in the Spirit and dare to say, we worship God in the Spirit; in which we only and ever rejoice in Christ Jesus as our life and our strength. That example, that personal witness to what God can do, is a promise. It gives us the divine assurance that what God did for Paul and his brethren, he can do for us. He asks nothing less of us, he will give it us.

The steps by which anyone can enter this life are simple and clear. There must be conviction and confession. If there be the least sense in our heart that our life has been more in the flesh than the Spirit, let us cherish that conviction. Let us give way to it, that the Holy Spirit may fully show us the evil of it as sin against God's grace. Let us not shrink from definitely confessing it before God. With all our experiences of grace in the past, let us be willing to confess this root of evil, and in confession throw it upon God to remove.

Then comes surrender and consecration. Surrender – the giving up of everything that is of sin or self into the death of the cross, so that with the old man crucified, the flesh and its lusts crucified, we may forsake all to follow Christ. For this we have no power – we hardly understand the words – but God, who led Christ through the cross to the resurrection. God will make us partakers of that death. Let us surrender ourselves to it and to him. He alone can, he surely will, make Christ live in us. Consecration will follow, as the willing sacrifice of the whole being to be holy to God and possessed by him, as the temple was holy to him and wholly devoted to his service alone, or as a sacrifice on the altar was holy, and wholly consumed to his glory.

Faith and rest are then the last steps. Faith in God, who does all. Faith in Christ, who gives the strength for the surrender, and undertakes to maintain it. Faith in the Holy Spirit, as given to be ours in his fullness, as now accepted and received by us, as flowing forth without ceasing from the living Lord to be each moment the breath and life of our life. And then rest, apart from light or feeling, in the confident assurance that the Three yet One God will do all in us.

The other steps are all subordinate. Faith is the one decisive step, in which the soul passes out of the life partly in the Spirit and partly in the flesh, and enters, in God's name and strength, upon a life and walk in the Spirit.

Will you not, my reader, join the company that by the grace of God say 'We are the circumcision, who worship in the Spirit of God and glory in Christ Jesus, and have no confidence in the flesh'? Kneel down and speak these words in faith. Dare to trust God that he enables you to live this life.

Chapter 13

The Inner Circle

'And he appointed twelve, that they might be with him, and that he might send them forth to preach.' Mark 3:14

The different measures of grace in believers here on earth have frequently been illustrated by the comparison of a series of circles round the central figure of our Lord. In the first or inner circle are found those whose watchword has been the closest possible communion with and conformity to Christ. Among these the diversity of gifts and calling is very great. Some there are who have given themselves much to contemplation and worship, and have so learnt the secrets of the divine life, that their utterances come with heavenly power through the ages to their brethren. And some, many of them simple and unknown people, have devoted themselves to the ministry of intercession, and, in the effectual, much-prevailing prayer of the righteous, have brought strength and blessing to those around them, or to future generations. Others, again, have, amid the duties of daily life, received grace to keep their garments undefiled, and, in a life of humility and love, have so carried the savour of God's presence and power with them, that men have felt: Of a truth God is in them. And still others have thrown themselves with a Christlike devotion, into service for their fellow-men, and have been able to manifest the rare grace of intense devotion to work with the maintenance of a tender intimacy with our Lord Jesus. To them all belongs the blessing of having attained to a walk in unbroken fellowship in the unclouded light of God's face.

Around this circle there is a second, consisting of a great and ever-increasing number who have often heard the voices and sometimes seen the lives of the inner circle, and do exceedingly long to enter it. They have accepted the great and blessed truth that every child of God is to live for God and the service of his kingdom in his measure, with as whole-hearted devotion as Christ did, but are burdened by the same continual disappointment. They still live in the region of struggle and effort. The full secret of faith, that faith to which is given streams of living water flowing out of it, they have not yet found. Amid many blessed experiences of God's grace they are not yet satisfied – the rest of faith is not yet theirs. But they, many of them, are pressing on – faint, yet pursuing – and will, in God's good time, enter the inner circle. For them specially the thought of a revival in which to bless believers has infinite attractions. When God's Spirit visits and quickens his people, he will find in them prepared hearts. The work they are now doing, and that not without blessing, will then be found to have been only the time of apprenticeship, fitting them to be wise master builders.

The third circle is a much larger one. In it are found multitudes of honest, earnest Christians, who desire to live and work for God, and yet know little of what it is to be spiritual men and women, or to strive after the perfection of Christian maturity. Through lack, perhaps, of spiritual teaching, or of a spiritual environment in the Christian life into which they were born, it cannot be said of them that their faith groweth exceedingly, or that men take knowledge of them that they have been with Jesus. The defect in their inner life is twofold. They know that they are saved, and acknowledge that out of gratitude they ought to live and serve the Lord who redeemed them. But this service is still a second and a secondary thing, to which they may devote as much of their time and strength and money as pleases them. They have never understood that he who came to give all, to live and die for them, asks, most earnestly and most justly, that their whole heart, with its love and interest, that their time and strength be devoted to his work and kingdom. With this there is the other defect, that they have never learnt what the power of Jesus is to save from sinning and from wandering, to keep the soul by his strength, in his will and in his love. Because there has not been a surrender to live entirely, every moment for him, the faith and the experience of unceasingly being kept by him is impossible. What reason for all these our brothers and sisters to join with us in the fervent prayer for revival in his church, and a revelation by his Spirit of these two simple things – what God actually wishes his children to be, and what he has undertaken to make them.

And then comes the outer circle, pausing on its out-skirts into the world, from which so many who are in it are hardly distinguishable. The chief feature of the Christian in this class is selfishness and worldliness. He is content with the hope of being saved. His great aim is to make the best of both worlds. He hopes for happiness in heaven, and seeks for happiness on earth, from very much the same motive. He may be regular in his church-going, and ready to take part in any collection for Christian objects as part of the work of the church to which he belongs. His chief interest in life is this present world, and its spirit is his spirit. The seed of the new life that he may have received at conversion is hindered from growing up or bearing fruit by the cares or the pleasures of this world. And the thought of revival, if not entirely strange, is limited to the idea of special efforts that sometimes may be made to bring others to the same Christianity he enjoys – the hope of going to heaven at death. But as for personal communion with God, delight in secret prayer or Bible study, the longing for the love of Jesus, or holiness, or power to save others – to all these thoughts he is a stranger. The prayers for revival for the church and believers he cannot understand. What reason that all of us, to whom God has given some insight into this need, and some desire for his blessing to be poured out, should plead for these as if we saw ourselves in this sad position, and cry to God that every child of his, who has indeed been born of the Spirit, might be so visited and quickened as to know something of his love and the joy of his salvaton.

The truth of there being an inner circle and its object is illustrated by what we see in our own body. It possesses two sets of organs, the one for the maintenance of its own life, the other for communication with the outer world. To the former belong the brain, the lungs, the heart, the digestive organs. The latter consist of eyes, ears, mouth, hands and feet. The former are by far the more important. Take away all the latter and a man can still live. But remove any one of the organs by which life is maintained and death ensues. And so among the members of Christ's body there are some wholly set apart to the maintenance of close communion with heaven and drawing down supplies for the use of the whole body. We do not want the body to be all brain and lungs, and yet we see how much more essential these vital organs are than those with which we do our work in the outer world. And so there are saints, often misjudged and condemned because they do not take the same part as others in Christian activities, or unknown by reason of poverty or simplicity or obscurity, who are indeed the living channels by which the life is kept flowing in those around them.

The objection to an inner circle is the fear that it may give rise to a Christian caste. It never can as long as scriptural teaching concerning it is understood. For one thing – that it knows no fence or gate. It is free to all – yes more, all are urged to enter in. The weak things, and the foolish things, and the base things, and the things that are despised and the things that are not, hath God chosen; none are excluded, except those that exclude themselves by reason of their wisdom and strength and glory. No man can exclude or admit: it is Christ himself who chooseth his own and whose Spirit ministereth to every man as he will. As little need we fear that it will weaken the obligation resting on all to live wholly for God, or the faith in the possibility of being able to be well pleasing to him. This life in the inner circle is so much a gift, connected with natural character, or special guidance in Providence, or favouring circumstances, or direct invitation of God's Spirit, that there can be no question of merit, or superior holiness. The only difference is not in obligation, but in grace that has pleased to give them a special calling to fill up that which is lacking in their brethren. And this faith in our safety against the cast idea lies in what Scripture teaches so emphatically that such special nearness to God and power with him is not granted for any selfish enjoyment or exaltation, but only and wholly for the benefit of the favoured members of the body. The historian Eusebius speaks of there being two ways of living. The one, being wholly separate from the ordinary conversation of common life, is devoted solely to the worship of God, through an exceeding degree of heavenly love. They who are of this order seem dead to the world, and are in their minds dwelling in heaven. From there, like so many citizens of heaven, they look down on human life making intercesssions and oblations to God almighty for the whole race of mankind. The highest exercises of the Christian life are the sacrifices they offer to God, imploring his mercy and favour for themselves and their fellow creatures. In the spirit of true self-sacrifice they live only for others.

It is not sufficiently noticed that our Lord gathered such an inner circle round himself on earth, and that many of his commands, which are sometimes applied to all who seek salvation, and therefore must be explained away, were literally meant for those who were ever to be and to share with him, and so to be set apart wholly for his work. When Christ said 'If any man will come after me, let him deny himself and take up his cross and follow me,' 'Whosoever he be of you that renounceth not all that he hath cannot be my disciple,' he spoke of a literal renouncing all and coming after him to go about and be as he was. It was only in close, intense, continual fellowship with himself, demanding the sacrifice of every other work or interest, that he could fit them for the work he had for them to do. And so it is still given to some to be drawn, sometimes without their knowing or understanding it, into such separation from what to others in most lawful or even most sacred duty, that with time and opportunity in close, continuous contact with the Lord, they may be so filled with the life of heaven that they may have much to impart to others. The church of our day needs nothing so much as a large number of men and women whose whole bearing and walk bear witness that the power of God can rest upon us, that God's presence can still make men see and confess of a man that God is manifestly with him.

It is of great importance that this truth of an inmost circle should be known and acknowledged. It will lead us to recognise in those whom God often calls to suffering, or poverty, or humiliation to fit them for it, the honour he puts upon them, and not to grudge their liberty if they withdraw from other paths. It will help to encourage some to see that a door is open to the very highest work for those who appear shut out from work they fain would do, or have to refuse work others would fain put upon them. It will be to some, who never may have thought of it, who are masters of their own time and means, a call to enquire whether they have ever considered that their liberty from other duties is not meant to be a liberty to be like the angels in heaven, and to be ministering spirits sent out to minister to the heirs of salvation. Above all, it will, in connection with our prayer for revival, remind us of what is really the greatest need of the church – men and women so entirely given up as living sacrifices for their fellow-men, so fully conscious of the work to be done in heaven, not only by intercession, but still more by receiving, in all its intensity and fullness the power of the divine life and love into themselves to impart to others. It will teach us to pray that God himself would seek and find intercessors, in number and power hitherto unknown, and set them as watchmen, with the command and the power, not to rest, until he makes his church a joy on the earth. God hasten it in his time!

I have spoken thus at length of the inmost of the four circles, because I feel deeply that as we see what the highest work is that a revived church will be able to do, we shall the better know what it is that we need to pray for for every believer. Nothing less than this – that entire, undivided devotion to God's work of saving men is the calling of each of his redeemed ones. For not one was a less price than the blood paid. For not one has less been wrought out than a full and complete deliverance. For not one is there any other path of service or blessing prepared than that of being wholly his who paid such a price, and witnessing of him with the whole heart and strength. As this truth is restored in the church, hearts will be prepared to know why revival is needed, what the whole tithe is that God looks for, and what the Holy Spirit may be expected and counted upon to work in those who are ready to give all. The need of the heathen world is so tremendous, the impossibility of the work being done unless there be an entire change in the present rate of devotion in men and women and money is so absolute, we are so sure that the sin of robbing God in not giving 'the whole tithe' will be visited with the withholding of blessing in our churches, that the truth ought to be proclaimed with trumpet sound. God asks every believer to live wholly for him. Bring men, however ignorant or impotent they feel as to carrying it out, to see and admit this; it will be the true preparation for the floods of blessing.

And to none will the message of the inner circle and its possibilities be more welcome than those who surround it in the second. God has during these last years been working in the hearts of many a longing desire for the fullest possible experience of his sanctifying and enabling grace and the fullest possible medium of fruitfulness in his service. They have had the vision of their high calling here in the world, even as the Son was sent of the Father, to live as the sent ones of Christ, only and solely to do the Father's will. They have not hesitated to accept that calling, and taken upon themselves the vows of an absolute consecration. They are giving themselves, and not without success, to work for fellow-men. Many of them have, in connection with God's work on earth, taken on them the vow, 'If God will show me anything that I can do for the evangelization of the world that I have not yet done, of his grace I will endeavour to do it at once.' And yet there are so many questions and difficulties. God has not shown them what more he would have them do. And yet they are conscious that there is so much more that they might do, if they knew how. And yet they have not entered that rest which they know is promised, and which comes when the Holy Spirit reveals fully Christ Jesus in the perfect completion of that work he undertakes so entirely and unceasingly to do within us. Let us gather with all such before the throne, and cease from ourselves in the quiet stillness of the faith that God will work all in us. The final blessing of our Lord Jesus is so to fill with the Holy Spirit that rivers of living water flow out of us. Let there not be the shadow of a doubt that the revival will bring this to many. We bring the whole tithe: God will open the windows of heaven, and pour out the exceeding abundant blessing.

And not only those who are prepared, but many who have not even sought will share it. Do let us believe that even as we who know what God demands, cannot count upon the personal blessing without the personal faithfulness, so as intercessors the blessing of those we pray for depends upon our faithfulness too. We have the power to confess, and to believe for others. Let us study the different states of those around us, the various stages of earnestness or formality, of honest purpose or worldly indifference, and so identify ourselves with our brethren who are sick, and in prison, and in darkness, that their need will indeed be as our own, and our prayers indeed as their own. Ever able and willing to give streams in the desert and rivers in the dry ground. Let us believe and intercede.

Chapter 14

Blessed to be a Blessing

'Now the Lord said unto Abram, Get thee out of thy country ... unto the land that I will shew thee ... and I will bless thee ... and be thou a blessing ... and in thee shall all the families of the earth be blessed' Genesis 12:1–3

Abraham is the father of all who believe; they are all called the children of Abraham. As such we are expected to do the works of our father Abraham, and to walk in the steps of that faith which he had. The faith by which he obeyed God, and went out not knowing whither he went, the faith which was counted unto him for righteousness, the faith which was made perfect by works, and gave glory to God, even to the sacrifice of what was dearer than life, is set before us as the pattern we ought to imitate. The more we go back to the first beginnings of God's dealings in grace with mankind as they are seen in him, and trace God's work to their roots and first principles, the clearer will our vision become of what God's purpose with us actually is. In the fuller and wider revelation of the New Testament we are in danger of confounding the essential with the secondary, and of resting content with elementary truths without really or fully grasping God's purpose with us.

In the very first words God spoke to Abram, we have a simple summary of God's will with every believer. The simple words, 'I will bless thee' contain the seed of all that the redemption of Christ can teach of God's love through time or eternity. They reveal the heart, the will, the work of the God in whom we are to believe, the God whose nature and power and delight it is to bless with every spiritual blessing. The words that follow, 'and be thou a blessing,' express as simply all that God aims at with the believer in blessing him. They tell us that just as God loves to be a blessing to his creatures, so his children are to have the honour, and privilege, and power of living for nothing less, being unceasingly a blessing to those around them. At man's creation God said, Let us make man in our image, after our likeness. Here to Abraham God shows wherein that likeness is chiefly to consist: even as God blesses, so he is to bless. 'In thee shall all the families of the earth be blessed.' He was to know that all God did for him, and all he did for God, was not to end in himself, but to be a blessing to his children, and through them to all the nations of the earth. This was to be the true blessing of God: the power, like God, to be a blessing.

A tree carries into every branch, and leaf, and fruit the nature of the seed from which it grew. Every child of Abraham, every believer, is as dependent upon God's blessing as Abraham was, is as sure of it in its quickening power as Abraham was, and is also meant in his measure to be a blessing as much as Abraham was. 'What God hath joined together, let no man put asunder.' The two parts of God's gracious will, the being blessed by God, and the being a blessing to others, are inseparable. God's blessing is only given to be passed on, to lift us into the fellowship and likeness and glory of God, in life spent, if need be consumed, in dispensing blessing.

And yet how few Christians there are who really believe this, who really believe in God for this. How few who really see the truth, or claim the privilege, or rejoice in the assurance that such a life is equally an obligation and a possibility. Many believers have never yet accepted the twofold truth: All God's blessing to me is meant for others; for all blessing I am to bring to others, God's blessing will fit me. We are treating of revival, of a quickening of a feeble life that has lost its power. We are praying for a restoration of scriptural religion. Surely we can do nothing better than study the Abraham type of piety, and beseech God to raise up children to him who do his work and walk in his steps. It is only when we 'bring the whole tithe' to God, and prepare to live wholly as he would have us, to be a blessing to men, so that his house may be filled, that we can expect the windows of heaven to be opened, and such blessing that there shall not be room to receive. Come, and let us study the lesson of this word which lies at the root of Abraham's life of faith. God is willing by his Holy Spirit to speak it in power into our hearts as he did into Abraham's.

1. God seeks for men and women through whom he can bless the world. When God created man in his image, it was that he, like God, might be the king and ruler of the world – God's viceregent. When man fell, and God began the great work of restoring the human race, he proved that man was still to hold his place, and that all his saving work was to be done through men. He did indeed, from time to time, send angels with his messages – but the real work of leading and blessing men was committed to men. Man was to be saved and blessed by man. It was for this the Son of God had to become man, and now sits as man on the throne. By man came death, by man comes life. And so today God needs, and seeks, men and women through whom he can bless the world.

Never in the history of the world was there such need of men as today. Think of two-thirds of the world, a thousand millions of heathens and Muslims, not knowing Christ. And only 17,000 men and women gone out to fight the awful power of Satan under which these souls are perishing. Think of the millions in Christian countries, some with their educated and even refined infidelity, others with their hard and profligate materialism, still others with a formal and dead religiousness. Think of the multitudes of Christians sleeping in worldliness and self-contentment. Think of so many more who are in earnest in trying to be saved and yet have no conception of the duty or the possibility of being a blessing to the world. And say, is there not a need of men like Abraham, who give themselves in the absolute surrender of faith for God to fill them with the power of his blessing and send them forth to bless? God has no way of blessing the world but through men filled with himself. God has no way of revealing himself in power in his church, or in heathendom but by men and women who are full of him, and carry his presence with them. God seeks for men and women through whom he can bless the world.

2. God asks that these men, and women, shall be wholly devoted to him. It was this God asked of Abraham. God's very first word to him was that he should separate himself from his country, and his kindred, and his Father's house, and get him into a strange land, there to walk alone with God, 'get apart for himself.' In faith Abraham gave himself away to God, looking for and trusting to, desiring and willing nothing but what God was and said and did. God was all, God was enough to him. And so God filled him with his blessing, and the blessing of Abraham has come upon us who receive the Spirit by faith.

God still seeks men utterly given up to him, whom he can so fill with his blessing, in its divine power, that men shall come to them because they see that God is with them. Of such devotion to God the majority of Christians have not the remotest conception. Their thought of religion is that they must make sure of having their sins pardoned, and of doing their best to live a Christian life. And then, if they give something for their church, and possibly for missions, they have done all that can be expected. There are many others, who are more earnest in their desire to please God both in their walk and in work for him, but who consider it impracticable in their circumstances to live so wholly and closely with God as always to be a blessing.

I come with the message that God longs and seeks for men and women wholly given up to him, whom he can fill with blessing for their fellow-men. He wants those whom he can fill with such a faith in his love for souls, with such a sense of the reality of hell and heaven, with such an experience in themselves of his power to bless and to save, that their testimony shall compel men to listen. God calls for such. Who will say, Here am I?

3. God's plan with such is, to fill themselves first with his blessing. Because this is not understood or believed, there is so much feebleness and failure in Christian work. Christians say that if one preaches the truth, a blessing is sure to come. This is far from true. When Christ promised the power of the Holy Spirit (Acts 1:8) he said, 'And ye shall be my witnesses.' A witness for Christ is one who, whether he speak of himself or not, gives evidence by his tone, by his life, by his power in the midst of weak Christians, that Christ lives, that Christ is with him and in him. From Abraham downwards to the Apostles God has shown that he wants men filled with his Spirit, possessing and proving his blessing, through whom he will bless and save. As he is the living fountain, and gives what he is and has himself, he enables us too to have the stream of living waters flow out the well of water within us.

What God asks in those he is thus to fill is nothing but this, that they be empty of all else. Be it home or friends, be it men or things, be it the world, or self, with an Abrahamlike readiness all must be sacrificed to make room for God, and entire devotion to him. Into such a soul he can freely pour his blessing and come himself to dwell and work. In the peace that proves all understanding, in the humility that proves a life ever in God's presence and fear, in the experience of his power to save and keep from sin, in the intensity of surrender to think and live for his kingdom, in the power of God's Spirit manifested in weakness, in a Christlike love and joy in seeking the lost, God will prove to the whole-hearted believer, and in him to others, that the world is divinely and unchangeably true: I will bless thee.

4. God's blessing thus received reveals the secret of true work for others to others. A spiritual insight into the far-reaching meaning of God's promise to Abraham and his seed would work a revolution in many an earnest minister and worker. It would mean something like this. Know that you can only impart in power what you are receiving fresh from God day by day. See that all you teach, and wish to see, in those to whom you speak is first truly and fully done in yourself. Live in the continual experience of God's supernatural blessing and Spirit in your own heart, and seek to say, What I have, I give thee. Do not attempt to give what you have not got; give as God gives you. The Word of God is the assurance that this is his will and order: I will bless thee, be thou a blessing. This dependence upon God, this surrender to being blessed of him, will work a holy confidence that we have the power to bless. We shall understand what it means: My strength is made perfect in weakness. We shall see how we are only to be channels, living channels indeed, and yet only channels, most honoured and blessed channels, conveying the blessing God is streaming into us to men around us. And we shall know in all our work to keep up the communion with God, who gives the blessing to us, as clear and close as with those to whom we carry it.

What a privilege thus to become the recipient and the bearer and the dispenser of the life and Spirit and power of God. What a change from sighing to joy, from the burden of duty to the liberty of faith, from the strain of effort to the rest of dependence, from failure to fruitfulness, would come into the life of many a worker, if they believed this and took Abraham's place before God. God seeks for men and women to do this, that he may fill them with the blessing of his life, and love to carry to men. Why should not every one who reads this say, Here am I, send me?

I return again to the great lesson of this book. If we are to pray for revival, if we are to know what the revival is we need, if we are to prepare ourselves for revival, if we are to bring the whole tithe into God's house, do let us remember that what God seeks is this – the whole heart and the whole life given up to be filled with his blessing, for the sake of bringing blessing to the perishing millions. And let each of us accept God's promise to Abraham in the faith that by his Holy Spirit God can make his Word living and active, working effectually in him that believes. Come and take your place as a true child of Abraham.

You have been asking for a blessing for yourself long enough. Begin today by saying: 'Lord! I give myself to thee, to use me, to consume me if need be in blessing the world. I desire to offer myself to thee, even as thy blessed Son did, to live only and wholly at thy disposal for carrying thy love to men and women. I desire to forsake everything, and be entirely set apart for thee to use in thy work of rescuing the world from sin. I would walk with thee, and wait on thee, until thou hast filled me with thy unquenchable love to sinners, and I know no joy but seeing men saved. Lord, fulfil in me the word: Be thou a blessing.

And then say: As I give myself to thee to work for thee, I give myself to thee to work in me. I count on thee to make the word true in me, and I will bless thee. O my Father, let my heart and life be so full of thy blessing, that it may overflow to others. Let my own experience of thy saving presence and power, thy blessed indwelling and love, be so clear and childlike, that in all simplicity and humility I may just show what God can do. O God of Abraham, visit your child, visit your people.

After God had said, Get thee out of thy country, I will bless thee and make thee a blessing, it is written: So Abraham went out, as the Lord had spoken to him. Let the obedience of faith mark our acceptance of God's promise. Let us ask him to show us the land of whole-hearted devotion, and the way into it. Let us at once undertake the journey. We can trust God to lead; we can be sure he will bless.

Christians, God seeks men and women through whom he can bless the world, people wholly given up to him. His name be praised that there are such in this age too, but all too few. Will you not join their number? Will you not say: I begin to see that no enthusiasm can be too great, no intensity of devotion too deep, no sacrifice too large, if I may be found worthy of being filled full every day with the blessing of God, and so made a blessing by him, for his kingdom and glory.

Chapter 15

The State of Illumination

'My prayers; … that the God of our Lord Jesus Christ, the Father of glory, may give unto you a spirit of wisdom and revelation in the knowledge of him; Having the eyes of your heart enlightened.' Ephesians 1:16–18

The saints of olden times often spoke of a state of illumination in the Christian life, without which it was not possible fully to know or do God's will. Our text was one of the many passages in God's Word they referred to. Paul had spoken (Eph. 1:13) of the believers having been sealed with the Holy Spirit of promise, as the earnest of their inheritance. He proceeds at once to tell them of his unceasing prayer that God might give them a Spirit of wisdom and revelation in his knowledge, having the eyes of their hearts enlightened. They must not think it enough that they had the Holy Spirit within them, as the earnest of their inheritance. No, what they had was only an earnest or pledge of all the heritage they could count upon. The first part of this, what they first of all needed, was to ask and receive from the Father the special gift of a Spirit of wisdom and revelation to enlighten the eyes of their heart in the knowledge of God, so that they might spiritually apprehend all that God had prepared for them.

It is not enough that a child be born into the world in the possession of all the wonderful faculties with which God has endowed man. In addition to this, he needs an education, an outside help, to draw out and guide and develop the faculties he possesses. Even the believer, sealed with the Holy Spirit of promise, to know that he is God's child, needs for his education and growth to know his dependence upon a divine enlightening of the heart, to enable him to know God and his Word, Christ and his grace aright. This is one of the chief causes of the feebleness of the spiritual life, even when there is the sealing of the Spirit, and the joyful assurance of being God's child, that the promise and power of the divine illumination is not known. Men are taught and dealt with as if, when once converted, they had in themselves the power to know the will and the grace of God in his Word. The increasing dependence upon a divine teaching from heaven, as alone sufficient to reveal heavenly things and to make heavenly-minded Christians, has not the place in the teaching of the church that it has in that of the Epistle. The very first thing Paul does, after speaking about them having believed and received the Holy Spirit, and before entering, in chapter 2, on the exposition of the new life they had received, is in his wonderful prayer, Eph. 1:15–23, to tell the wonderful things which without the divine Spirit of enlightenment they could not possibly know or possess aright.

I have more than once in this volume spoken of the lack of the acknowledgement of the Spirit's teaching, and the consequent trust in man's wisdom, as one of the chief causes, not only of the sickly life, but of the failure of appeal or testimony to effect a change. The calling of the believer is so divine and supernatural, the blessedness which may be his position here on earth is so spiritual and heavenly, and the power that can work in him is so truly omnipotent and therefore beyond our reason, that the clearest intellectual conceptions utterly fail to grasp them. In this great prayer of the apostle, then, three points are there of which he speaks in connection with the divine illumination of the Spirit. Unless we learn to believe in this, to wait for it, and every day to live our life under its guidance, we cannot rise to the full height either of the calling, the heritage, or the power of the Christian life. Under these three headings all Paul's teaching can be comprised.

1. Our Calling. 'That ye may know the hope of your calling.' The word calling has special reference to the object for which we have been called. We are called to be saints. Paul was called to be an Apostle. We are called unto peace, unto liberty, unto eternal glory. Both of patience in suffering, and love towards our enemies, Peter says: hereunto were ye called. Our calling is spoken of as holy, a high and heavenly calling. God hath not called us unto uncleanness, but unto holiness. The epistle to the Ephesians begins its practical part by saying, 'Walk worthy of the calling wherewith ye were called, with all lowliness and meekness, with longsuffering.' And Paul describes his own life as a pressing onward towards the goal unto the prize of the high calling of God in Christ Jesus. That included both his calling to a saint, and a servant, his call to the fellowship and the service of Jesus Christ.

When we speak of a man's calling in this life, we understand the profession, or trade, or occupation to which he devotes himself and his time. The more thoroughly men and women understand their calling and the more heartily they give themselves to it, the more likely are they to succeed. Paul knows how essential this is, and so he asks for these believers the indispensable special revelation of the Holy Spirit of what their calling is, what the object is for which God has called them out of the world. It includes the calling both to be saints and the calling to service. In both respects the enlightening of the Holy Spirit in our days is as much needed as with the days of the Ephesians.

We are called to be saints. We are called unto holiness. It is strange how little the words 'saints' and 'holiness' are used in the ordinary language of Christians. Various reasons may be given for this, all partially true. But the chief one must be the divine grace they express. The fruit of the indwelling of the Spirit of holiness is too little known. Holiness is the very essence and being of God; this is why his Spirit is called the Holy Spirit. Holiness is the work of what belongs to, is owned and possessed by God. Holiness is savour of the divine presence resting on man, the separatedness from the world, the heavenliness which proves a man's close communion with God. It combines the cleansing from all defilement of the flesh and spirit, with obedience to all the commandments and the fulfilment of all righteousness. But through and above this it receives the very disposition and likeness of Christ Jesus, the holy one of God.

We need the Holy Spirit's enlightening of the heart for more than one reason. He only can show what God's standard of holiness is. He only can discover how much there is in our ways of thinking and acting which, though not condemned by man may not and need not be. He only can reveal how sufficient the provision for making us holy, and how certain its bestowal will be. We need a revival of holiness in the church.

And as we are called to be saints so also be servants. We all admit this easily. But few understand it – to be a bondslave of Jesus Christ, bound to him by a willing, fervent love. And yet this is what he asks. And what he needs, too, if his work is ever to be done in the world. All that is said about the duty of the church to the world, Christian or heathen, falls comparatively powerless for lack of a spiritual apprehension. When the Holy Spirit shows how unceasing and blessed is the privilege, how urgent the duty and the need of giving all one's life to the glorious work of winning men to Christ, and inspires the heart with the love and the faith that does it, our calling in the world will become something, higher than heaven is above earth, more glorious than it ever has been to us.

2. Our Heritage. 'What the riches of the glory of his inheritance in the saints.' Obligation and privileges always go together. The calling refers to the duty of the Christian and what God asks of him. The heritage points to the blessing God bestows. Some have thought that the word here is used of the inheritance which God has in the believer. I can hardly think this. Five verses previously, the Spirit was spoken of as the earnest of our inheritance, suggesting that it is his work to show in what that inheritance is. The terms 'riches of glory', are generally used to denote what God bestows on us. (See Eph. 1:6–7; 2:7; Phil. 4:19). The two other points on which the revelation is needed deal with the inner life of the Christian. All this appears to debar the other and more unusual application of the term. The believer needs to know the wonderful riches of grace and glory of which, as an heir of God, a fellow-heir with Christ, he has become the possessor in this life. Only then can he by faith inherit the promises.

And what is now the riches of the glory of God's inheritance of which his saints are the possessors? Riches on earth suggest the thought of the payment of every debt, the supply of every need, sufficiency to satisfy every desire, and abundance to overflow to others. The inheritance of the child of God includes all this. From every debt and every unfulfilled obligation he has been set free, as he became heir of the infinite and inexhaustible righteousness of Christ. For every need there is an inexhaustible supply in Christ our treasury, of whom it is said: 'He came full of grace and truth, and out of the fulness we have received, grace for grace.' And there is more than just the mere supply of every need: 'God is able to make all grave abound toward you, that ye having always all sufficiency, may abound unto every good work.' Every desire of the soul can be fulfilled. And so exceeding abundant are these riches of grace that there is enough to impart to all liberally and in full measure. The riches of the Father are all at the disposal of the heir, who accepts the leading of the Spirit to bring him into the promised inheritance. God's child is meant to live as the son of a rich Father, who giveth all things richly to enjoy.

To look at the inheritance from another side. It includes the love of God – not only his grace and favour, but his love resting on and delighting in his child, and revealing itself in closest communion. It embraces the peace and joy of God, filling the heart, and bringing down heaven to earth. It gives access to the wisdom and all the attributes of God, surrounding the believer with the light of God's perfections. To a man who uses his riches aright, they give a sense of nobility and influence. A child of God who knows his inheritance can go through the world, scattering blessing with unstinted hands, for he knows that of these divine riches the chief glory is that the more we give the richer we become.

How differently God's children would live if they knew 'the riches of the glory of their inheritance.' How blessed the state of illumination in which the Holy Spirit enlightens us to know and possess the things which God hath freely given us. Every promise would come to us with the vision of an infinite God waiting to fulfil it. Every need and desire would be accepted as the divine premonition of what God was to work. Our life and walk would be in the heavenlies, and we should live blessed with all spiritual blessings in heavenly places in Christ Jesus. Let us plead fervently for the Spirit of wisdom and revelation that enlightens us to know all this – a wonderful revival will surely follow.

3. Our Prayer. 'And what the exceeding greatness of his power to us who believe, according to that working of the strength of his might which he wrought in Christ, when he raised him from the dead, and made him to sit

at his right hand in the heavenly places.' Lest anyone should say, The high calling is too high, I cannot attain to it, the inheritance is too glorious, it is not for this world. The Holy Spirit meets our unbelief at once by speaking of the divine, the omnipotent power that is to work all this in us. We can walk worthy of our calling; we can through faith inherit the promises; in proportion to the calling and the inheritance is the power God has provided. The power that works in us is none other than the resurrection power which our Lord was raised from the dead to the throne of glory. If anything the spirit of revelation is needed, it is here – for the discovery and the faith of the power of God that is working in them. Our calling is so heavenly and the life we are to live is so supernatural; our inheritance is so spiritual, and so beyond the grasp of human apprehension, that it is only by the operation of a divine, an omnipotent power, beyond all our thought or expectation, that God's purpose with us can be fulfilled. God himself alone can work all things according to the purpose of his will. The power of God alone is commensurate with the purpose of God. And the Spirit alone is able to reveal in us what the purpose and the power are.

As in God's plan so in our experience these two things may not be separated. The power will only be given fully to work in the man who accepts the purpose. As long as we take our human views of what appears possible or reasonable, we see in vain the words of Paul's prayer. When we accept the Spirit's teaching on the holiness of our calling and the heavenly nature of the inheritance God gives in us, he will assuredly reveal the mighty power that is needed and is waiting. This is the very first condition for receiving the Spirit's revelation of the power of God – be ready in its strength to live up to the habit of your calling. Receive a supernatural power for an altogether supernatural life.

The second is, receive it as a resurrection power – a power that raises from the dead. It was this in Christ: it can be nothing but this in us. As we enter into Christ's death to sin, and self, and the world, as we know that we are dead in him, and carry about his dying in our mortal body and carry out that dying in our dead life, the power of his life can work in us. We know him in the power of his resurrection, being made conformable to his death.

And the third condition is faith. Enlightened eyes of the heart to know the exceeding greatness of his power to us *who believe*. It must be a life of faith. In dying Christ committed his Spirit into his Father's hands, and so entered the helplessness of death and the grave. He counted on God to raise him up. And so we need to be brought off from all our efforts, and all our hopes of doing something better, to cast all upon God, and believe that by God's omnipotence working in us, we can live up to our calling and the riches of our inheritance. As the Holy Spirit shows us this death to all that is of self and of nature, and the working of the power of God's might which he wrought in Christ, working in us, we shall have the courage to believe that we can indeed walk worthy of our calling.

Would not a fulfilment of the prayer in Ephesians 1:15–20, be in itself a blessed revival, the very revival we need? Let us make that prayer a definite part of our prayer for revival. That the need of the Holy Spirit's enlightenment may be felt, that the certainty of his being given and of his effectual teaching may be believed, that the true calling, and heritage, of the believer, with the mighty, inner working of God's power in him, may be known – let this be made a matter of earnest, persevering prayer in a church or circle of friends – God will not withhold the same.

The Africa Evangelical Fellowship

The AEF is an international evangelical mission. For more information about their work, please contact them at their International office, 17 Westcote Road, Reading, Berks RG3 2DL.

The AEF has hundreds of opportunities for both long and short term service in evangelism, church planting, education, medical administration, youth work and other practical fields.

Other AEF offices are:-

Australia
PO Box 292
Castle Hill
New South Wales 2154

Zimbabwe
99 Gaydon Road
Graystone Park
Borrowdale
Harare

Canada
470 McNicoll Avenue
Willowdale
Ontario M2H 2E1

South Africa
Rowland House
6 Montrose Avenue
Claremont 7700

USA
PO Box 2896
Boone
North Carolina 28607

New Zealand
PO Box 1390
Invercargill

United Kingdom
30 Lingfield Road
Wimbledon
London SW19 4PU

Europe
5 Rue de Meautry
94500 Champigny-sur-Marne
France